JAMITO FAMILY TREE

Tatay Jobo Elizes
2011

Jamito Family Tree
Edited & Published by Tatay Jobo Elizes
Edition, 2011
Copyright

ISBN-13: 978-1463578527
ISBN-10: 1463578520

Publisher
Tatay Jobo Elizes
2011

Dedication

This book is dedicated to all members of the Jamito Family Tree.

Acknowledgment

Special thanks is reserved to Belen Jamito-Ramores Aguilar-Buan, my Elemenary classmate, Calss 1947. She belongs to Branch No. 6 of the Jamito Clan. She gave me the original listing which I used in creating the website. I also give thanks to those members who emailed me the corrections and additions to the listing.

Publisher - Tatay Jobo Elizes

Contents

(Surnames here: Alarde + Aquino + Abrera + Asis + Baay + Bamba + Belmonte + Bual + Cayanan + Curioso + Dizon + Egar + Erum + Gache + Gutierrez + Ibanez + Ipanag + Jamito + Naldo + Magana + Mago + Maria + Ramirez + Ramos + Rico + Rivera + Rosales + Santiago + Sechin + Vargas + Villaluz + Zabala + Zaldua)

(Surnames here: Abina + Abuyo + Abrera + Alvarez + Baay + Basto + Cortez + Damayo + Dimaranan + Ellazar + Jamito + Juan + Manalo + Mendoza + Rocelle + Sacriz + Sacueza + Tan + Tolentino + Travilla + Ubana + Valles + Villamonte)

Publisher - Tatay Jobo Elizes

(Surnames here: Abolencia + Abordo + Abrera + Abuyo + Agleran + Agot + Amante + Ang + Angeles + Apin + Arrojo + Aspe + Balce + Balata + Bamba + Borja + Brando + Cabanela + Cacho + Cambronero + Capistrano + Cayno + Cereno + Coballes + Correa + Cortez + DelaCruz + Diaz + Domingo + Elep + Esperas + Embestro + Farlan + Gache + Gadil + Gallardo + Garido + Glipo + Godeloson + Gonzales + Gravador + Ibana + Ibanez + Ibeas + Ignacio + Jamito + Llames + Lonto + Lou + Magana + Magtibay + Maigue + Manlangit + Mapol + Mariano + Marquesas + Marquez + Mercado + Naesa + Nieva + Orendain + Pancho + Pango + Pardo + Pedir + Perez + DelaPunta + Quibral + Rada + Rafer + Rafon + Ragiles + Rala + Ramores + Ramos + Rana + Rasco + Rayos + Relles + Reyes + Rivera + Roldan + Rojas + Sanchez + Sta.Ana + Seminiano + Simeon + Sinaon + Teodoro + DelaTorre + Ubaldo + Valerio + Valles + Vargas + DeVera + Villa Garcia + Villanea + Yuson + Zaleta + Zantua + Zenarosa)

Branch No. 4 - Jamito-Barilla p. 42

(Surnames here: Abejero + Abello + Abrina + Abuyo + Acop + Aguirre + Alba + Albonia + Arevalo + Arines + Asur + Atienza + Bacolor + Barbosa + Barreto + Barilla + Basa + Bautista + Bongate + Borromeo + Botardo + Bueno + Bemata + Cabanela + Cabale + Cabonce + Cabriano + Callo + Camacho + Campomanes + Cano + Caramoan + Carino + Casis + Castro + Cavinte + Cootauco + Crucero + Cruz + DelaCruz + Cuano + Cubinar + Dalupang + Denny + Diaz + Dimas + Din + Dionisio + Echavez + Eco + Efa + Efondo + Eliazo + Elizes + Ella + Escalante + Espeleta + Estanislao + Estrada + Fajardo + Fernandez + Ferrer + Francisco + Freyra + Getuya + Gonzales + Gonzalvo + Gregorio + Guerrero + Gurea + Hart + Hernandez +

Herrera + Hollinger + Hollmann + Ibeas + Icatlo + Iglesias + Jamo + Javier + Jerson + Dejesus + Jimenez + Jones + Kath + Kimmeth + Laban + Labordo + Lax Amana + Legaspi + Deleon + Leondra + leslie + Licerio + Licas + Llago + Lorenzo + Lou + Maesa + Magana + Magyawe + Makalintal + Manlangit + Manly + Maras + Marcelo + Marcilla + Mase + Mercado + Miguel + Miranda + Mission + Moquia + Mozada + Murallo + Obusan + O'Malley + Omoto + Overa + Pamesa + DePanis + Panong + Pajares + Paqueo + Parente + Parian + Pascual + Pena + Pena Florida + Purinque + Querubin + Quirubin + Quijano + Rada + Rafer + Ragasa + Ragos + Ramirez + Ramores + Rasco + Recondo + Redondo + Sanchez + Delos Santos + Sarabillo + Savilla + Serrano + Sia + Sicat + Soliven + Soriano + Talay + Thompson + Timbalopez + Trapane + Troso + Ubana + Uya + Valerio + Valeros + Varin + Victa + Villa + Villa Luna + Villaluz + Viloria + Yao + Yap + Yogore + Yulo + Zantua + Zenarosa + Zurbano)

Branch 5 - Jamito-Ubina   p. 71

(Surnames here: Abonal + Acituna + Alconcel + Agravent + Altoviros + Angeles + DelosAngeles + Aragon + Avila + Babin + Bacuno + Balice + Barrios + Bellen + Benoza + Bernal + Bitonio + Bockhop + Brinas + Buan + Caballero + Caramoan + Castillo + Chavez + Chua + Conley + Consuelo + Contreras + Cosio + Cruz + DelaCruz + Cuano + Dator + Dietrich + Ebuenga + Ella + Espana + Eva + Fermo + Flores + Galero + Garde + Gaskell + Gerio + Gomez + Gonzales + Guardian + Guinto + Gutierrez + Imperial + Jacobo + Jamito + Jimenez + Joaquin + Lacey + Largo + Las + Legaspi + Macalino + Madronio + Magana + Mancenido + Malises + Marian + Marquez + Moreno + Nicolas + Ocampo + Orbillo + Pabico + Padilla + Palado + Pempena + Pena + Pulido +

Publisher - Tatay Jobo Elizes

Puso + Quia + Quinto + Rafer + Ragiles + Ramores + Ranada + Raymundo + Rayos + Reales + Rebodos + Roco + Rodriguez + Rosales + Leprosaria + Rudaje + Sabularse + Salazar + Sales + Santos + Tapales + Torres + Ubina + Ursolino + Valenzuela + Vargas + Velasco + Villa Garcia + Villaluz + Villapoma + Villarosa + Yanilla + Young)

Branch 6 - Jamito-Ramores p. 91

(Surnames here: Abina + Abital + Abrera + Abriol + Abuyo + Aciado + Adating + Aguilar + Albonia + Aloc + Amado + Anaya + Anson + Aragon + Arevalo + Asis + Avelinia + Avellana + Baay + Bajane + Maldonado + Balthazar + Barizo + Barieta + Baron + Barosa + Baynosa + Bongalon + Borac + Braga + Brazos + Buan + Cabingan + Cacho + Calag + Callada + Calubayan + Cama + Cambay + Camborne + Cariaga + Casis + Cayabyab + Clabe + Clacio + Colan + Cortez + DelaCruz + Cuaderes + Cubinar + Cuevo + Daniel + Decena + Diaz + Durante + Edoria + Efa + Efondo + Egar + Encina + Espana + Espinar + Fernandez + Filio + Florante + Florentes + Francisco + Freyra + Gache + Gacho + Gadil + Galina + Gallardo + Gamier + Garcia + Gasis + Gomez + DeGuzman + Hernandez + Ibana + Ibis + Ilaan + Jalina + Jamito + Jerez + Dejesus + Jovan + Lallo + Lascano + Lavarro + Deleon + Libria + Lopez + Mabesa + Mabeza + Maesa + Magana + Mago + Mariano + Martillan + DeMata + Melendez + Mislana + Morales + Oliva + Oltazar + Orendain + Ortiz + Pada + Pascua + Pedir + Penaranda + Penaredondo + Pieza + Piquant + Pixcio + Placido + Plza + DelaPunta + Puzon + Racho + Ramos + Ramores + Rampas + Rana + Sacriz + Salidong + Salva + Sanchez + Santos + DelosSantos + Sarical + Sarmiento + Savilla + Sayno + Seminiano + Seville + Tabor + Teodoro + Tibor + Ubana + Vanan + Villa + Villanueva + Villarosa + Wabon + Yanesa + Yanto +

Ybarola + Zantua)

Sub - Branch - Jamito-Ragiles-Jamito   p. 111

(Surnames here: Abad + Abordo + Abungan + Acabado + Adones + Asido + Asis + Baay + Barnedo + Baser + Benamira + Bentulan + Biguera + Bucalbos + Cabatsa + Cabutotan + Canela + Castillo + DelaPunta + Delarosa + DeVera + DelosAngeles + Delos Santos + Derry + Dinglasan + Elep + Enofrio + Espanola + Fausto + Gapoy + Gonzales + Goyala + Ibis + Jalimao + Jamito + Kataoka + Leano + Leviste + Ling + Lorenzana + Luster + Magada + Mago + Malijan + Mercurio + Molina + Montes + Motola + Muit + Mujal + Nava + Neri + Ogada + Ojas + Oseo + Pabico + Pascua + Pensacola +Polycarp + Rada + Ragiles + Ramos + Reyes + Rudolph + Saberola + Salcedo + Sanchez + Segundo + Tamayo + Tan + Tuzon + Ubana + Uriarte + Velarde + Vergara + Verona + Villacrusis + Villafranca + Villagarcia + Villamor + Villanueva + Yanela + Zafe)

Publisher's List   p. 124

Publisher - Tatay Jobo Elizes

Foreword

Publishing a book about the Jamito Family Tree became necessary because there are still many people who do not use computers, internet and emails. Many do not know that the Jamito Family Tree is in the internet and has a website, under www.jamitotree.webs.com, that the publisher created more than 5 years ago. It continues to be updated due to ease and convenience.

This book is mostly listing of names and their coded positions in the family tree. We have included email messages from some members regarding corrections to the listing. We encourage such comments and corrections to be included in future editions. Maybe, we can include stories too.

We realize this book is not prefect and there would be errors of listing, years of birth or death, spelling of names, etc. We encourage submissions of suggestions how to improve this book.

In this family tree, the assigned codes are permanently assigned and will never change in future editions. It is therefore easy to find them. One must know his/her particular branch in the tree.

This family tree will contiue to grow as more additional names are included, due to non-inclusion during this first edition. Also, more births will occur in the future.

I may need the assistance of volunteers or helpers. Please email the publisher.

This book is a good guide for everybody. Every family and members should have a copy.

Publisher - Tatay Jobo Elizes

JAMITO HERITAGE

FAMILY TREE LISTING OF DESCENDANTS IN SIX OR SEVEN GENERATIONS FROM 1830s.

SANTIAGO JAMITO
PATRIARCH, 1830s

This is a genealogical history of the Jamito Clan from Talisay, Camarines Norte, Philippppines, starting from the

Patriarch, SENOR SANTIAGO JAMITO

and Matriarch, SENORA JACOBA MAGANA,

from mid 1800's generation up to 2000s.

Organized by JOBO GUERRERO ELIZES, Code JB.5.1.1.2. of the Branch No. 4 -under SEVERINO JAMITO + APOLINARIA BARILLA Clan.

Majority of the data collected herein were supplied by BELEN RAMORES AGUILAR-BUAN, Code JR.2.1.3. of Branch No. 6 - under ANA JAMITO + RUFINO RAMORES Clan.

Contact: job_elizes@yahoo.com

Publisher - Tatay Jobo Elizes

PAGHAHANDOG
Written in Tagalog by 3 oldest members
of the clan, who were past 90 years of age in 2001, when
they signed this document, namely:

DOMINGA JAMITO RAMORES-AGUILAR, JR.2.1.(RIP),
BEATRIZ JAMITO ABRIOL-PADILLA, JU.4.1. (RIP), and
PAZ JAMITO RAGILES-MARQUEZ, JU.2.6. (RIP)

Ang kasaysayang ito ay handog namin sa lahat ng mga kasapi sa Nobenaryo ng "NUESTRA SENYORA DEL ROSARIO" hanggang sa mga darating pang mga kaapu-apohan nina Sr. SANTIAGO JAMITO at Sra. JACOBA MAGANA sa bayan ng Talisay, Camarines Norte.

Originally Assembled & Prepared By:
BELEN RAMORES AGUILAR-BUAN, JR.2.1.3.
at MARTINA JAMITO-CABANTING, JI.3.1.5.

SALAMAT SA DIYOS, dahil sa loob ng tatlong daan at limampung (350) taon ng mga Castila sa Pilipinas, pagmamahal sa Diyos ang ipinama sa atin. Ito ay katangi-tangi sa bayan ng Talisay, Camarines Norte.

Ang pagdarasal sa Santo Rosario araw-araw ay isang makadiyos na gawain ng mag-asawang Sr. Santiago at Sra. Jacoba. Sila ay taal na taga Talisay at naging Patron nila ang nuestra Senora Del Rosario. Ang magasawang Sr. Santiago Jamito at Sra. Jacoba Magana ay nabiyayaan ng anim (6) na anak. Ito ay sina:

(1) FROILAN JAMITO
(2) CLARO JAMITO
(3) AGATA JAMITO
(4) SEVERINO JAMITO
(5) BRAULIO JAMITO
(6) ANA JAMITO

Publisher - Tatay Jobo Elizes

Naisip ng mag-asawang Sr. Santiago at Sra. Jacoba na panatilihin ang mga pagkakabigkis ng pamilya, kaya't pinasimulan nila ang pagnonobena sa kanilang patron na Del Rosario. Ito ay nagsisimula Sabado pagkatapos ng fiesta ng bayan ng Talisay (Oktubre 4). Sa baro ng Santa (Del Rosario) ay may nakaburdang initial ng AMJ na ang ibig sabihin ay ANA MAGANA JAMITO. Iyan ang ibinurda ni Lola Jacoba sa damit ng Santa dahil binigyan niya ng bendisyon ang pinakabunsong anak na si Ana, na siya ang mangalaga ng Santa o Imahen ng Nuestra Senora Del Rosario at mangasiwa sa pagdarasal sa pagnonobena.

Ang mag-asawang Sr. Santiago at Sra. Jacoba ay may pag-aari sa nayon ng Gabon, Talisay, Camaraines Norte, ng dalawang sagip na bukirin. Ito ang pinagkukunan nila ng pangangailangan sa tuwing pagdiriwang ng taun-taon ng kanilang patron.

Pagkalipas ng ilang taon ay nagsipag-asawa na ang mga anak nila Sr. Santiago at Sra. Jacoba. Heto ang mga naging asawa ng kanilang mga anak:

> (1) Froilan Jamito + Gregoria Ibanez,
> (2) Claro Jamito + Estafania Abina,
> (3) Agata Jamito + Gregorio Valles,
> (4) Severino Jamito + Apolinaria Barilla,
> (5) Braulio Jamito + Michaela Ubina,
> (6) Ana Jamito + Rufino Ramores.

Ng magkaroon na ng kanya-kanyang pamilya ang mga anak nina Lolo Santiago at Lola Jacoba ay napagkasunduan na ang nobernaryo ay ipagpatuloy sa pamamagitan ng paghahali-halili o pagsalin-salin ayon sa pagkakasunod-sunod ng magkakapatid simula sa panganay hanggang bunso. Dahil sa anim lamang ang anak ni Sr. Santiago at Sra. Jacoba, napagkasunduan na ang tatlong malalaking pamilya ay hatiin para makumpleto ang siyam na araw ng pagdarasal o pagnonobena. Kaya't and pamilya Agata, Severino at Braulio ay nahati.

Ang dalawang sagip na bukirin na nabanggit sa itaas ay walang tunay na kasulatan o "deklarasyon" na magpapatunay na ito ay pag-aari ng buong pamilya sa dahilang malaki ang paniniwala ng ating mga ninuno na ang lupaing ito ay ipinagkaloob bg biyaya ng Mahal na Diyos. Napagkasunduan din ng mga magkakapatid na kung sino ang may pasiyam o kamarero ng noberya ng Nuestro Senora Del Rosario, ay siyang magsasaka o gagawa ng bukid na ito. Dito sa bukiring ito manggagaling ang pangangailangan o ipaghahanda ng nobenaryo.

Ang ating pamahalaan ay may kani-kanyang sangay. Mayroong tagapangasiwa ang bawat sangay at kailangan namang bigyan sila ng sahod. Nagkaroon din ang pamahalaan ng Cadastral Survey Team at noon lamang nagkaroon ng titulo ang lupaing ito ng mag-asawang Sr. Santiago at Sra. Jacoba. Nagkaroon ng kautusan ang pamahalaan na ipagbabayad ng buwis ang mga deklaradong lupa. Sa buwis ng mga lupain kukunin and ipagbabayad sa iba't-iang proyekto at sa tagapangasiwa ng pamahalaan. Dahil dito, napagkasunduan din ng magkakapatid na kung sino ang kamarero ay siyang magbabayad ng buwis ng lupaing ito at sila rin and gagawa o magsasaka ng dalawang sagip na bukiring ito.

Sa tulong ng tatlo (3) pang buhay na kasapi na buhat sa ikalawang henerasyon na sina Nana Dominga Ramores-Aguilar (96 yrs. old), Nana Bating Abriol-Padilla (93 yrs. old) at Nana Paz Ragiles-Marquez (92 yrs. old), ay naisakatuparan ang pagsusulat ng kasaysayang ito. Salamat na muli sa Poong Maykapal at idalangin natin na maipagpatuloy natin and debosyon ng ating mga ninuno o ang angkan ng Sr. Santiago at Sra. Magana-Jamito.

Ipanalangin natin na laong magkabigkis-bigkis, magka-isa, magmahalan, matahimik at mapayapa ang ating pagsasama-sama. Magkaisa tayong magpipinsan sa pamagitan ng pagdiriwang ng nobenaryo sa NUESTRA SENORA DEL ROSARIO, dated 2001:

Pinagtibay: **DOMINGA JAMITO RAMORES-AGUILAR (SGD), JR.2.1.(RIP)**

Pinagtibay: **BEATRIZ JAMITO ABRIOL-PADILLA (SGD), JU.4.1. (RIP)**

Pinagtibay: **PAZ JAMITO RAGILES-MARQUEZ (SGD), JU.2.6. (RIP)**

(English Translation)

THANK GOD, because for three hundred and fifty (350) years of Spanish rule in the Philippines, God bestowed love on us. It is exceptional in the town of Talisay, Camarines Norte. There is Santo Rosario prayer in everyday work of a godly couple, Sr. Santiago and Sra. Jacoba. They are indigenous to Talisay and they became devotees to Patron Saint Nuestra Senora del Rosario.

The spouses Sr. Santiago Jamito and Sra. Jacoba Magna had been blessed with six (6) children. They were:

(1) Froilan JAMITO
(2) Claro JAMITO
(3) Agata JAMITO
(4) Severino JAMITO
(5) Braulio JAMITO, AND
(6) ANA JAMITO.

Sr. Santiago and Sra. Jacoba kept the marriage bond and love of the family, and so they began their homage and prayers by reciting the novena to their Patron Saint Del Rosario. It usuasally started at Saturday after the feast of the town of Talisay (October 4). In the coat of Santa (Del Rosario) was embroidered initial of AMJ, that means ANA MAGANA JAMITO. Lola Jacoba did this embroidery as a form of blessings to the youngest daughter Hannah or Ana, who took care of the Image of Nuestra Senora Del Rosario and supervised the novena prayers.

The couple Sr. Santiago and Sra. Jacoba had owned lands in the village of Gabon, Talisay, Camaraines Norte, consisting of two pieces of rice fields (2 sagip). These fields yielded income which is the source they need every year to celebrate the novena and festival in honor of their Patron Saint Senora Del Rosario, as contribution of the whole family with great devotion.

After a few years, their children got married. Here are the espouses of their children:

Publisher - Tatay Jobo Elizes

(1) Froilan Jamito + Gregoria Ibanez
b(2) Claro Jamito + Estafania Abina
(3) Agata Jamito + Gregorio Valles
(4) Severino Jamito + Apolinaria Barilla
(5) Braulio Jamito + Michaela Ubina, and
(6) Ana Jamito + Rufino Ramores.

The family of Sr. Santiago and Sra. Jacoba, specially the sons agreed that the annual nobenaryo or novena prayers shall be held and will be managed by each of the 6 families. But to be able to complete the nine (9) novenas, additional families were needed. So it was decided that the bigger families shall be subdivided into 2 divisions in order to complete the compsition of nine novenas, to be managed alternately by ach of the nine family groupings. The oldest family shall be the first to start, followed by the younger ones in order of chronology. It took nine (9) years to complete the cycle. The 3 large families of Agata, Severino and Braulio were split into two each, for this purpose.

The two productive rice-fields mentioned above had no real titles or "declaration" of ownership, as they were handed down from generation to generation. It belonged to Jamito ancestors and that this land was granted by grace of God, the produce from which were traditionally used in the nine (9) novenas, or "pasiyam". They had agreed that the family who were assigned to handle the "pasiyam" for the given year, shall farm the 2 rice fields or agricultural lands in order to make them productive and earn the necessary funds. The funds were to be utilized for the novena prayers and festivals.

The Government has their respective divisions. There are different branches and administrators, whose expenses and wages are paid by the Govrnment. There was also the government of Cadastral Survey Team and then only had the title of this land for the couple Sr. Santiago and Sra. Jacoba. There was a law required by the government that land tax must be paid. Because of this, the family and the sons and daughters agreed that the family assigned for that particular year of novena shall take care of paying the land tax with income coming from the 2 lands mentined above.

Publisher - Tatay Jobo Elizes

As of this writing, the three (3) oldest living members of the Jamito clan from earlier generations are: (2001):

a) Nana Dominga Ramores-Aguilar (96 years old),
b) Nana Beatriz (Bating) Abriol-Padilla (93 years old), and
c) Nana Paz (Pang) Ragiles-Marquez (92 years old),

They had executed the writing of this history. Thanks again to God Almighty and we pray that we continue our devotion to our ancestors or the family of Sr. Santiago James and Sra. Jacoba Jamito.

Let us pray and continue to come together, love each other, through our serene and peaceful unification. We unite via our blood relationship for this novena festivals and prayers or "nobenaryo" in celebration of Nuestra Senora del Rosario.

----End of English translation----

GUIDE IN READING THE CODES:

FAMILY TREE IN CODED STYLE - NOT CHART-TYPE

JI - JAMITO-IBANEZ (FROILAN JAMITO + GREGORIA IBANEZ) - BRANCH 1

JA - JAMITO-ABINA (CLARO JAMITO + ESTEFANIA ABINA) - BRANCH 2

JV - JAMITO-VALLES (AGATA JAMITO + GREGORIO VALLES) - BRANCH 3

JB - JAMITO-BARILLA (SEVERINO JAMITO + APOLINARIA BARILLA) - BRANCH 4

JU - JAMITO-UBINA (BRAULIO JAMITO + MICHAELA UBINA) - BRANCH 5

JR - JAMITO-RAMORES (ANA JAMITO + RUFINO RAMORES) BRANCH 6

JRJ - JAMITO-RAGILES (TITO JAMITO + MARIA RAGILES). SUB-BRANCH

(Tito Jamito probably belongs to Patriarch Santiago's brothers or cousins. But significantly, his wife Maria Ragiles is sister to Placido Ragiles, son-in-law of Braulio Jamito+Michaela Ubina.)

One digit or number means 1st. generation;
Two digits or numbers - 2nd. Generation level
Three digits or numbers - 3rd. Gen.and so on.

Numeral 1 means 1st born;
Numeral 2 means 2nd born;
Numeral 3 means 3rd born, and so on.
nb - means no-blood relation.

Publisher - Tatay Jobo Elizes

GENEALOGY OR FAMILY TREE

ORIGINAL ROOT

SANTIAGO JAMITO + JACOBA MAGANA 1830s

Publisher - Tatay Jobo Elizes

BRANCH NO.1
FROILAN JAMITO +
GREGORIA IBANEZ
(JI - JAMITO-IBANEZ, 1850s)

Publisher - Tatay Jobo Elizes

JI.1. ALEXANDRA IBANEZ JAMITO, 1870s

JI.2. SIXTA IBANEZ JAMITO, 1870s, single

JI.3. JUAN IBANEZ JAMITO, 1870s + LUCIA RAMIREZ, nb
JI.3.1. SERGIO RAMIREZ JAMITO, 1890s + MENA ZALDUA, nb
JI.3.1.1. AUREA ZALDUA JAMITO, 1910s, + GUILLERMO BELMONTE, nb
JI.3.1.1.1. DR. JOSE JAMITO BELMONTE, 1930s, Army Doctor
JI.3.1.1.2. NORA JAMITO BELMONTE, 30s. Single, Nurse.

JI.3.1.1.3. DOUGLAS JAMITO BELMONTE, 30s, of Funeraria Belmonte
JI.3.1.1.4. THELMA JAMITO BELMONTE,40s
JI.3.1.1.5. EMELITA JAMITO BELMONTE, 40s
JI.3.1.1.6. WILLIAM JAMITO BELMONTE, 40s
JI.3.1.1.7. ARTHUR JAMITO BELMONTE, 50s
JI.3.1.1.8. LEDNICKY JAMITO BELMONTE, 50s

JI.3.1.2. SEVERINA ZALDUA JAMITO, 1910s, RIP
JI.3.1.3. IRENEO ZALDUA JAMITO, 1920s, RIP

JI.3.1.4. VALERIANO ZALDUA JAMITO,1920s, RIP

JI.3.1.5. MARTINA ZALDUA JAMITO, B1930s - D2006/9/20, + EMILIO
RIVERA, H1, nb + MR. CABANTING, H2, nb - One author of Preface -
Paghahandog - Nobenaryo

JI.3.1.5.1. LIWAY JAMITO RIVERA, 50s + RUDY EGAR, nb
JI.3.1.5.1.1. JASMIN RIVERA EGAR, 70s
JI.3.1.5.1.2. JOEL RIVERA EGAR, 70s
JI.3.1.5.1.3. DENNIS RIVERA EGAR, 70s
JI.3.1.5.1.4. RODERICK RIVERA EGAR, 80s
JI.3.1.5.2. EMMA JAMITO RIVERA, 50s + VIRGILIO ASIS, nb

JI.3.1.6. PEDRO ZALDUA JAMITO, 30s, RIP
JI.3.1.7. OLIVA ZALDUA JAMITO, 30s + INOCENTES GAD ZABALA, nb

JI.3.1.7.1. HECTOR JAMITO ZABALA, '59 + SUSANA AUSTRIA, nb
JI.3.1.7.1.1. VAUGHN MARTIN ZABALA

JI.3.1.7.1.2. PATRICIA MAE ZABALA
JI.3.1.7.1.3. SYDNEY HARRY ZABALA
JI.3.1.7.1.4. LARA VICTORIA SUE ZABALA
JI.3.1.7.1.5. HARVEY ZABALA JI.3.1.7.1.6. HANS ZABALA
JI.3.1.7.1.7. HAILE SANS ZABALA
JI.3.1.7.1.8. SANDRA ZABALA

JI.3.1.7.2. LEA JAMITO ZABALA, '61 + UWE KOCH, nb, Germany.
(uk1950@yahoo.com Gabon,Talisay,
Name: Uwe koch + Lea Zabala-Koch
Email: uk1950@yahoo.com
Date: Tue May 22, 2007, Thank you very much for this great family-tree. I am the daugther of Oliva Jamito and Inocentes Zabala, married to a German and live also there. But soon we will live and stay for good in Gabon. Hope to meet many of yours during the next Del Rosario. God bless the Jamito-Clan)

JI.3.1.7.3. SARAH JAMITO ZABALA, '63 + JOSE VARGAS, nb

JI.3.1.7.4. MELANIE JAMITO ZABALA, '64 + AMADEO GENETIA, nb
JI.3.1.7.4.1. JENSKIN JOHN GENETIA
JI.3.1.7.4.2. DAYLANIE GENETIA JI.3.1.7.4.3. JOSHUA GENETIA

JI.3.1.7.5. RUBEN JAMITO ZABALA, '65 + DAISY VARGAS, '66, nb
JI.3.1.7.5.1. RUTH DESIREE ZABALA, DEC 2, 1994
JI.3.1.7.5.2. RENZ DELMOR ZABALA, FEB 2, 1997
JI.3.1.7.5.3. RAVEN DOROTHY ZABALA, NOV 27, 1999

JI.3.1.7.6. EDWIN JAMITO ZABALA, '65 + ANGELA BISOY, '65, nb
JI.3.1.7.7. ELWIN JOY ZABALA, '85

JI.3.1.8. MIGUEL ZALDUA JAMITO, 30s + ELVIE SANTIAGO, nb
JI.3.1.8.1. MICHAEL SANTIAGO JAMITO, 50s

JI.3.1.8.2. MICHELLE SANTIAGO JAMITO, 50s
JI.3.1.8.2. MAGIE SANTIAGO JAMITO, 50s

JI.3.1.9. AMADOR ZALDUA JAMITO, 40s + EMILIANA RICO, nb
JI.3.1.9.1. ROSALINDA RICO JAMITO, 60s + ROLANDO GUTIERREZ, nb
JI.3.1.9.2. JOSE RICO JAMITO, 60s + MARILYN NALDO, nb

JI.3.1.9.3. FROILAN RICO JAMITO, 60s + JOSEFA IPANAG, nb
JI.3.1.9.4. LORETA RICO JAMITO, 70s + RODOLFO DIZON, nb
JI.3.1.9.5. IMELDA RICO JAMITO, 70s + DANILO ERUM, nb
JI.3.1.9.6. MARIA THERESA RICO JAMITO,70s + SECHIN HERRERA, nb
JI.3.1.9.7. NERISSA RICO JAMITO, 70s + CLAURIS, nb
JI.3.1.9.8. AMADOR RICO JAMITO JR, 80s + AGRIPINA AQUINO, nb
JI.3.1.9.9. WILMA RICO JAMITO, 80s + CARLITO RAMOS, nb
JI.3.1.9.10. BASILO RICO JAMITO, 80s, rip

JI.3.1.10. ROMULO ZALDUA JAMITO, 40s + CARMELITA BAMBA, nb
JI.3.1.10.1. NOEL BAMBA JAMITO, 60s + ESMALINDA ROSALES, nb
JI.3.1.10.1.1. ELOISA ROSALES JAMITO, 80s
JI.3.1.10.2. NEIL BAMBA JAMITO, 60s + ALINA ALARDE, nb
JI.3.1.10.2.1. JUNEL ALARDE JAMITO, 80s
JI.3.1.10.3. MA.CARMELA BAMBA JAMITO, 60s + MANOLO MARIA, nb
JI.3.1.10.3.1. MARVIN JOSEPH JAMITO MARIA, 80s

JI.3.1.10.4. MARIA CHRISTINA BAMBA JAMITO, 70s + ARVIN BUAL, nb
JI.3.1.10.4.1. BRET MICHAEL JAMITO BUAL, 90s
JI.3.1.10.4.2. ERICA JAMITO BUAL, 90s

JI.3.2. PAULO RAMIREZ JAMITO, 1890s + ANGELA BAAY, W1, nb +
RAYMUNDA MAGO, W2, nb

JI.3.2.1. PAULINA BAAY JAMITO, 10s + FLORENCIO GACHE, nb
JI.3.2.1.1. BELLA JAMITO GACHE, 30s
JI.3.2.1.2. MYRNA JAMITO GACHE, 30s
JI.3.2.1.3. NORMITA JAMITO GACHE, 30s

JI.3.2.2. MAMERTO BAAY JAMITO, 10s, RIP
JI.3.2.3. LEVY JAMITO MAGO JAMITO, 20s
JI.3.2.4. VICENTE MAGO JAMITO, 20s + MERCEDES, nb
JI.3.2.4.1. MARCRIS JAMITO, 40s
JI.3.2.5. ERLINDA MAGO JAMITO, 20s + ERNESTO CAYANAN, nb

JI.3.3. FILOMENA RAMIREZ JAMITO, 1890s + MAXIMO VILLALUZ, nb
JI.3.3.1. JOSE JAMITO VILLALUZ, 10s

Jl.3.3.2. OSCAR JAMITO VILLALUZ, 10s
Jl.3.3.3. LILY JAMITO VILLALUZ, 10s + MR. DE VERA, nb

Jl.3.4. ANASTACIA RAMIREZ JAMITO, 1900s + CIRIACO CURIOSO, nb

Jl.3.4.1. GAVINA JAMITO CURIOSO, 20s, rip
Jl.3.4.2. JULIANA JAMITO CURIOSO, 20s
Jl.3.4.3. COSME JAMITO CURIOSO, 20s
Jl.3.4.4. ELEODORO JAMITO CURIOSO, 30s
Jl.3.4.5. PETRA JAMITO CURIOSO, 30s
Jl.3.4.6. PONCIANO JAMITO CURIOSO, 30s
Jl.3.4.7. PRIMO JAMITO CURIOSO, 40s

Jl.3.5. FRANCISCA RAMIREZ JAMITO, 1900s + PEDRO ABRERA, nb

Jl.3.5.1. ROMAN JAMITO ABRERA, 20s
Jl.3.5.2. LEONARDO JAMITO ABRERA, 20s
Jl.3.5.3. NEMESIO JAMITO ABRERA, 20s
Jl.3.5.4. ADELAIDA JAMITO ABRERA, 30s
Jl.3.5.5. RUFINA JAMITO ABRERA, 30s
Jl.3.5.6. LEANDRO JAMITO ABRERA, 30s

BRANCH NO. 2
CLARO JAMITO +
ESTEFANIA ABINA
(JA - JAMITO-ABINA, 1850s)

Publisher - Tatay Jobo Elizes

JA.1. SERAPIA ABINA JAMITO, 1870s + VICTOR MANALO

JA.1.1. REGINA JAMITO MANALO, 1890s + BASILIO BAAY, nb

JA.1.1.1. SEGUNDINO MANALO BAAY, 10s + CENONA BASTO, nb
JA.1.1.1.1. EMILIA BASTO BAAY, 30s + JOLITO LAGUMEN, nb
JA.1.1.1.2. NILDA BASTO BAAY, 30s + CAYO UBANA JR, nb
JA.1.1.1.2.1. PRINCESS LYNETH BAAY UBANA, 50s
JA.1.1.1.2.2. JOHN BAAY UBANA

JA.1.1.1.3. FERNANDO BASTO BAAY, 30s
JA.1.1.1.4. RENE BASTO BAAY, 40s
JA.1.1.1.5. LOLITA BASTO BAAY, 40s
JA.1.1.1.6. PIAMETA BASTO BAAY, 40s
JA.1.1.1.7. ERLINDA BASTO BAAY, 50s
JA.1.1.1.8. BESSIE BASTO BAAY, 50s

JA.1.1.2. VICTOR MANALO BAAY, 10s + PACITA AREVAL0, W1 + ANACITA ZANTUA, W2

JA.1.1.2.1. NOEMI AREVALO BAAY, 30s + MIGUEL ELLAZAR, nb
JA.1.1.2.1.1. GUILLERMO BAAY ELLAZAR, 50s
JA.1.1.2.1.2. BENJAMIN BAAY ELLAZAR, 50s
JA.1.1.2.1.3. ANALYN BAAY ELLAZAR, 50s

JA.1.1.2.2. NENITA ZANTUA BAAY, 40s + DIOSDADO TOLENTINO, nb
JA.1.1.2.2.1. DIOSDADO BAAY TOLENTINO JR., 60s + MELANIE VILLAMONTE, nb
JA.1.1.2.2.1.1. DION ANGEL VILLAMONTE TOLENTINO, 80s
JA.1.1.2.2.2. DENNIS BAAY TOLENTINO, 60s
JA.1.1.2.2.3. DARWIN BAAY TOLENTINO, 60s

JA.1.1.2.3. VILMA ZANTUA BAAY, 40s + ARTURO TRAVILLA, nb
JA.1.1.2.3.1. OWEN FELIX BAAY TRAVILLA, 60s + ANNIE ROSA SANDURTA, nb
JA.1.1.2.3.1.1. JANICIA SANDURITA TRAVILLA, 80s

JA.1.1.2.4. RUBEN ZANTUA BAAY, 40s + ERLINDA CORTEZ, nb
JA.1.1.2.4.1. MAYLYN CORTEZ BAAY, 60s
JA.1.1.2.4.2. SONIA CORTEZ BAAY, 60s
JA.1.1.2.4.3. JOEL CORTEZ BAAY, 60s
JA.1.1.2.4.4. ERWIN CORTEZ BAAY, 70s
JA.1.1.2.4.5. AILEEN CORTEZ BAAY, 70s

JA.1.1.2.5. BELLA ZANTUA BAAY, 50s + MANUEL ABRERA, nb
JA.1.1.2.5.1. MARVIN BAAY ABRERA, 70s
JA.1.1.2.5.2. HAZEL BAAY ABRERA, 70s
JA.1.1.2.5.3. NOEL BAAY ABRERA, 70s
JA.1.1.2.5.4. CYRENE ANN BAAY ABRERA, 80s
JA.1.1.2.5.5. MANUEL BAAY ABRERA JR, 80s

JA.1.1.2.6. VICTOR Z. BAAY, 50s + JOSIE SACRIZ, nb
JA.1.1.2.6.1. MICHAEL SACRIZ BAAY, 70s
JA.1.1.2.6.2. JOEL SACRIZ BAAY, 70s

JA.1.1.2.7. NESTOR ZANTUA BAAY, 50s + CRISTINA ROCELLE, nb
JA.1.1.2.7.1. SHIRLEY ROCELLE BAAY, 70s
JA.1.1.2.7.2. CHRISTOPHER ROCELLE BAAY, 70s
JA.1.1.2.7.3. SHUELA ROCELLE BAAY, 70s
JA.1.1.2.7.4. CARMELA ROCELLE BAAY, 80s
JA.1.1.2.7.5. MARICRIS ROCELLE BAAY, 80s

JA.1.1.2.8. ANTONIO ZANTUA BAAY, 50s + REMEDIOS DIMARANAN, nb
JA.1.1.2.8.1. REMY ANNE DIMARANAN BAAY, 70s
JA.1.1.2.8.2. MARK ANTHONY DIMARANAN BAAY, 70s

JA.1.1.2.9. ELEANOR ZANTUA BAAY, 60s + ARNEL TAN, nb
JA.1.1.2.9.1. MA.CHRISTINA BAAY TAN, 80s
JA.1.1.2.9.2. ARNEL BAAY TAN JR, 80s
JA.1.1.2.9.3. MARY ELEANELLE BAAY TAN, 80s
JA.1.1.2.10. MARLENE ZANTUA BAAY, 60s + LUISITO DAN JUAN, nb
JA.1.1.2.10.1. LORIELYN BAAY JUAN, 80s
JA.1.1.2.10.2. JOHN LOUIE BAAY JUAN, 80s
JA.1.1.1.10.3. MARK XAVIER BAAY JUAN, 80s
JA.1.1.3. JOSE MANALO BAAY, 10s + GREGORIA ABUYO, nb

Publisher - Tatay Jobo Elizes

JA.1.1.3.1. LENIDA ABUYO BAAY, 30s + JUAN ALVAREZ, nb
JA.1.1.3.1.1. ESTRELLA BAAY ALVAREZ, 50s
JA.1.1.3.1.2. RONNIE BAAY ALVAREZ, 50s
JA.1.1.3.1.3. RICARDO BAAY ALVAREZ, 50s
JA.1.1.3.1.4. ERLINDA BAAY ALVAREZ, 50s
JA.1.1.3.1.5. RENE BAAY ALVAREZ, 60s

JA.1.1.3.2. EDEN ABUYO BAAY, 30s + ROGELIO SACUEZA
JA.1.1.3.2.1. RUBEN BAAY SACUEZA, 50s + MINERVA ABINAL, nb
JA.1.1.3.2.1.1. MARYBETH ABINAL SACUEZA, 70s
JA.1.1.3.2.1.2. NINA ABINAL SACUEZA, 70s
JA.1.1.3.2.2. EDDIE BAAY SACUEZA, 50s + CRISTINA
JA.1.1.3.2.2.1. MAESA SACUEZA, 70s

JA.1.1.3.2.3. MYRA BAAY SACUEZA, 50s + TEODORO DAMAYO, nb
JA.1.1.3.2.3.1. IAN JEFFREY SACUEZA DAMAYO, 70s
JA.1.1.3.2.3.2. PAOLO NIEL SACUEZA DAMAYO, 70s
JA.1.1.3.2.4. MARY JANE BAAY SACUEZA, 60s
JA.1.1.3.3. EDUARDO ABUYO BAAY, 30s
JA.1.1.3.4. REGINA ABUYO BAAY, 30s
JA.1.1.3.5. NANCY ABUYO BAAY, 40s + ARTEMIO MENDOZA, nb
JA.1.1.3.5.1. MERINE BAAY MENDOZA, 60s
JA.1.1.3.5.2. MANUEL BAAY MENDOZA, 60s
JA.1.1.3.5.3. ERNESTO BAAY MENDOZA, 60s

JA.1.1.3.6. ALEX ABUYO BAAY, 40s
JA.1.1.3.7. RODEL ABUYO BAAY, 40s
JA.1.1.3.8. FREDDIE ABUYO BAAY, 40s
JA.1.1.3.9. ARNEL ABUYO BAAY, 50s + SHIRLEY
JA.1.1.3.10. ANITA ABUYO BAAY, 50s

JA.1.1.4. SIMEON MANALO BAAY, 20s + ALUDIA VALLES, nb
JA.1.1.4.1. ERLINDA VALLES BAAY, 40s

Publisher - Tatay Jobo Elizes

BRANCH NO. 3
AGATA JAMITO +
GREGORIO VALLES
(JV - JAMITO-VALLES, 1850s)

JV.1. FRANCISCA JAMITO VALLES, 1870s + FELIPE DELA PUNTA, nb

JV.1.1. FELICIANO VALLES DELA PUNTA, 1890s + NEMESIA CAYNO, nb

JV.1.1.1. MELANIO CAYNO DELA PUNTA, 10s

JV.1.2. ANDRES VALLES DELA PUNTA, 1890s + CRISANTA UBALDE, nb

JV.1.2.1. ESTER UBALDE DELA PUNTA, 10s + ROMEO RASCO, nb
JV.1.2.2. EMILDA UBALDE DELA PUNTA, 10s + JOSE GACHE, nb
JV.1.2.3. EMILIANA UBALDE DELA PUNTA, 10s + ROMUALDO REYES, nb
JV.1.2.4. ELER UBALDE DELA PUNTA, 10s + LILIA NAESA, nb

JV.1.2.4.1. MARILOU NAESA DELA PUNTA, 30s + EUGENIO ROJAS, nb
JV.1.2.4.1.1. BRYAN JOSEPH DELA PUNTA ROJAS, 50s
JV.1.2.4.1.2. FATIMA DELA PUNTA ROJAS, 50s

JV.1.2.4.2. MELCHOR NAESA DELA PUNTA, 30s + DINA CAMBRONERO, nb
JV.1.2.4.2.1. DINDIN CAMBRONERO DELA PUNTA, 50s
JV.1.2.4.3. MELVIN NAESA DELA PUNTA, 30s + ELENITA PEREZ, nb
JV.1.2.4.4. ROLAND NAESA DELA PUNTA, 40s

JV.1.2.5. VICTOR UBALDE DELA PUNTA, 20s + CARMEN IBANA, nb
JV.1.2.6. JOSE UBALDE DELA PUNTA, 20s + ALELI BALCE, nb
JV.1.2.7. ELISA UBALDE DELA PUNTA, 20s + APOLINAR GRAVADOR, nb
JV.1.2.8. ELISEO UBALDE DELA PUNTA, 20s + TERESITA DOMINGO, nb

JV.1.2.9. ANTONIO UBALDE DELA PUNTA, 30s + LEONORA IBEAS, nb
JV.1.2.10. EFREN UBALDE DELA PUNTA, 30s + MERLY LLAMES, nb

JV.1.3. PAULO VALLES DELA PUNTA, 1890s + SOLEDAD VARGAS, nb

Publisher - Tatay Jobo Elizes

JV.1.3.1. ELISA VARGAS DELA PUNTA, 10s + FERNANDO ABORDO, nb
JV.1.3.2. AUGUSTO VARGAS DELA PUNTA, 10s + LUISA LONTO, nb
JV.1.3.3. LOLITA VARGAS DELA PUNTA, 10s + JULIO MERCADO, nb
JV.1.3.4. ARTEMIO VARGAS DELA PUNTA, 10s + AURELIA MAIGUE, nb
JV.1.3.5. NILDA VARGAS DELA PUNTA, 20s + JUAN VILLAGARCIA, nb
JV.1.3.6. RENATO VARGAS DELA PUNTA, 20s + AMELIA SEMINIANO, nb

JV.1.3.6.1. RODEL SEMINIANO DELA PUNTA, 40s + ROSIE RAFER, nb
JV.1.3.6.1.1. RALPH JAYSON RAFER DELA PUNTA, 60s
JV.1.3.6.1.2. HERMINIA RAFER DELA PUNTA, 60s
JV.1.3.6.1.3. AMYREN RAFER DELA PUNTA, 60s

JV.1.3.7. NESTOR VARGAS DELA PUNTA, 20s + MERCY
GODELOSON(nb)
JV.1.3.7.1. MILVEN GODELOSON DELA PUNTA, 40s
JV.1.3.7.2. MELBA GODELOSON DELA PUNTA, 40s

JV.1.3.8. EMMA VARGAS DELA PUNTA, 20s + MARIO ESPERAS, nb
JV.1.3.8.1. ERWIN DELA PUNTA ESPERAS, 40s
JV.1.3.8.2. ERNANI DELA PUNTA ESPERAS, 40s
JV.1.3.8.3. BRENDA DELA PUNTA ESPERAS, 40s
JV.1.3.8.4. JOY DELA PUNTA ESPERAS, 50s

JV.1.3.9. ISABELO VARGAS DELA PUNTA, 30s + ALICIA CORREA, nb
JV.1.3.9.1. MICHAEL CORREA DELA PUNTA, 50s
JV.1.3.9.2. JOMER CORREA DELA PUNTA, 50s
JV.1.3.9.3. JONATHAN CORREA DELA PUNTA, 50s
JV.1.3.9.4. MARIA CRISTINA CORREA DELA PUNTA, 50S
JV.1.3.9.5. EUGENE CORREA DELA PUNTA, 60s
JV.1.3.9.6. CRISTINA JOY CORREA DELA PUNTA, 60s

JV.1.4. ALEJANDRO VALLES DELA PUNTA, 1890s + TRINIDAD GACHE, nb, W1 + MARINA MAIGUE, W2, nb

Publisher - Tatay Jobo Elizes

JV.1.4.1. CORAZON GGACHE DELA PUNTA, 10s
JV.1.4.2. BELEN GACHE DELA PUNTA, 10s
JV.1.4.3. CARLOS GACHE DELA PUNTA, 10s
JV.1.4.4. LEONORA GACHE DELA PUNTA, 20s
JV.1.4.5. TITA MAIGUE DELA PUNTA, 30s
JV.1.4.6. TERESA MAIGUE DELA PUNTA, 30s

JV.1.5. ENCARNACION VALLES DELA PUNTA, 1900s + GEORGE IBEAS, nb

JV.1.5.1. RUDY DELA PUNTA IBEAS, 20s + SHIRLEY, nb
JV.1.5.2. EDUARDO DELA PUNTA IBEAS, 20s + MATILDE, nb
JV.1.5.3. WILFREDO DELA PUNTA IBEAS, 20s + MANUELA, nb
JV.1.5.4. HENRY DELA PUNTA IBEAS, 30s + EVELYN, nb
JV.1.5.5. DANIEL DELA PUNTA IBEAS, 30s
JV.1.5.6. ELIZABETH DELA PUNTA IBEAS, 30s + RENATO, nb

JV.2. ARISTON JAMITO VALLES, 1870s + SOFIA MAGANA, nb

JV.2.1. BEATRIZ MAGANA VALLES, 1890s + EUGENIO MARIANO, nb

JV.2.1.1. VERONICA VALLES MARIANO, 10s
JV.2.1.2. LAUREANA VALLES MARIANO, 10s
JV.2.1.3. ALEJANDRA VALLES MARIANO, 10s
JV.2.1.4. CESAR VALLES MARIANO, 20s
JV.2.1.5. PAZ VALLES MARIANO, 20s

JV.2.2. ANICETA MAGANA VALLES, 1890s + TIMOTEO CACHO, nb

JV.2.2.1. GREGORIA CACHO VALLES, 10s + LEON RIVERA, nb
JV.2.2.1.1. DELIA VALLES RIVERA, 30s + RODULFO GAMBAL, nb
JV.2.2.1.2. BENJAMIN VALLES RIVERA, 30s + VIOLETA RECODO, nb
JV.2.2.1.2.1. JESSIE RECODO RIVERA, 50s + MARCIANA NAVARRO, nb

JV.2.2.1.2.1.1. JOHN MICHAEL NAVARRO RIVERA, 70s
JV.2.2.1.2.1.2. RICHELLE ANN NAVARRO RIVERA, 70s
JV.2.2.1.2.1.3. MARK JOSEPH NAVARRO RIVERA, 70s
JV.2.2.1.2.1.4. JESSICA MAE NAVARRO RIVERA, 80s
JV.2.2.1.1.1.5. MARIANNE JOY NAVARRO RIVER, 80s

JV.2.2.1.2.2. MARIBETH RECODO RIVERA, 50s, rip
JV.2.2.1.2.3. ROMEO RECODO RIVERA, 50s + MARCELITA LAZARRO, nb
JV.2.2.1.2.3.1. JENNY LAZARRO RIVERA, 70s. JV.2.2.1.2.3.2. KIMBERLY
LAZARRO RIVERA, 70s
JV.2.2.1.2.3.3. NICOLE LAZARRO RIVERA, 80s

JV.2.2.1.2.4. GEMMA RECODO RIVERA, 50s + PAMFILO ENTICO, nb
JV.2.2.1.2.4.1. MA. ANGELA RIVERA ENTICO, 70s
JV.2.2.1.2.4.2. BEN ART RIVERA ENTICO, 70s.
JV.2.2.1.2.4.3. KING J RIVERA ENTICO, 80s

JV.2.2.1.2.5. FRANCIS RECODO RIVERA, 60s + JOCELYN SURNAME, nb
JV.2.2.1.2.5.1. JOHN PAUL RIVERA, 80s
JV.2.2.1.2.5.2. JEFFREY RIVERA, 80s
JV.2.2.1.2.6. GLENDA RECODO RIVERA, 60s + JOSELITO BUENO, nb
JV.2.2.1.2.6.1. JHONNA RIVERA BUENO, 80s
JV.2.2.1.2.6.2. ANGELA LOVETTE RIVERA BUENO, 80s
JV.2.2.1.2.6.3. AJ RIVERA BUENO, 80s

JV.2.2.1.2.7. ALONA RECODO RIVERA, '78 + HENRY ZANTUA GASIS,
(JB.8.2.4.12), 60s. Home: Bicutan, Taguig City. Work: DOST-SEI. Graduate: BSIT, PUP-Taguig Campus. alon5665@yahoo.com)

JV.2.2.1.2.7.1. FIONA EUNICE RIVERA GASIS, 00s

JV.2.2.1.3. NORMA VALLES RIVERA, 30s + EMPLING BAUTISTA, nb
JV.2.2.1.3.1. ELMER RIVERA BAUTISTA, 50s
JV.2.2.1.3.2. ELER RIVERA BAUTISTA, 50s
JV.2.2.1.3.3. AIDA RIVERA BAUTISTA, 50s
JV.2.2.1.3.4. RUBEN RIVERA BAUTISTA, 60s

JV.2.2.1.4. CARMEN VALLES RIVERA, 40s

JV.2.2.1.5. IMELDA VALLES RIVERA, 40s
JV.2.2.1.6. MARIA VALLES RIVERA, 40s
JV.2.2.1.7. RAMON VALLES RIVERA, 40s + HELEN SURNAME, nb

JV.2.2.1.7.1. MARCH RIVERA, 60s
JV.2.2.1.7.2. CRISTY RIVERA, 60s
JV.2.2.1.7.3. ROY RIVERA, 60s

JV.2.2.2. FILOMENA CACHO VALLES, 10s + VENTURA RAGILES, nb
JV.2.2.2.1. ROSALINA VALLES RAGILES, 30s + MANUEL RAYOS, nb
JV.2.2.2.1.1. RODEL RAGILES RAYOS, 50s
JV.2.2.2.1.2. RAUL RAGILES RAYOS, 50s + ARVIE AGLERAN, nb
JV.2.2.2.1.2.1. JOAN AGLERAN RAYOS, 70s
JV.2.2.2.1.2.2. DIANNE CRISELDA AGLERAN RAYOS, 70s
JV.2.2.2.1.2.3. JONALYN PEARL AGLERAN RAYOS, 70s

JV.2.2.2.1.3. ROSALIE RAGILES RAYOS, 50s + ROY SANCHEZ, nb
JV.2.2.2.1.3.1. MARU RAYOS SANCHEZ, 70s
JV.2.2.2.1.3.2. RIZZA RAYOS SANCHEZ, 70s

JV.2.2.2.1.4. RICARDO RAGILES RAYOS, 60s
JV.2.2.2.1.5. ROWENA RAGILES RAYOS, 60s
JV.2.2.2.1.6. ROSABEL RAGILES RAYOS, 60s
JV.2.2.2.1.7. MANUEL RAGILES RAYOS JR, 70s

JV.2.2.2.2. NENITA VALLES RAGILES, 30s + BENJAMIN ARROJO, nb
JV.2.2.2.2.1. ARIEL RAGILES ARROJO, 50
JV.2.2.2.2.2. AILEEN RAGILES ARROJO, 50s + ARCHIE YUSON, nb
JV.2.2.2.2.2.1. ARVIN EDUARDO ARROJO YUSON, 70s

JV.2.2.2.2.3. ANITA RAGILES ARROJO, 50s

JV.2.2.2.3. JOB VALLES RAGILES, 30s + ZENAIDA PARDO, nb
JV.2.2.2.3.1. JOWEN PARDO RAGILES, 50s
JV.2.2.2.3.2. GINA PARDO RAGILES, 50s + MICHAEL ASPE, nb
JV.2.2.2.3.3. JEANETTE PARDO RAGILES, 50s
JV.2.2.2.3.4. JOY PARDO RAGILES, 60s
JV.2.2.2.3.5. JOB PARDO RAGILES JR, 60s

Publisher - Tatay Jobo Elizes

JV.2.2.2.4. LEVY VALLES RAGILES, 40s + TERESITA AGOT, nb
JV.2.2.2.4.1. EMMA AGOT RAGILES, 60s + MOISES IBANEZ, nb
JV.2.2.2.4.1.1. MALYN RAGILES IBANEZ, 80s
JV.2.2.2.4.1.2. ELMAR RAGILES IBANEZ, 80s
JV.2.2.2.4.1.3. JASON RAGILES IBANEZ, 80s
JV.2.2.2.4.2. ELMER AGOT RAGILES, 60s
JV.2.2.2.4.3. EDUARDO AGOT RAGILES, 60s
JV.2.2.2.4.4. ARLEEN AGOT RAGILES, 60s
JV.2.2.2.4.5. ALEXIS AGOTRAGILES, 70s
JV.2.2.2.4.6. BELLA AGOT RAGILES, 70s + DANNY RELLES, nb
JV.2.2.2.4.7. MELANIE AGOT RAGILES, 70s
JV.2.2.2.4.8. MAYLEEN AGOT RAGILES, 70s

JV.2.2.2.5. AIDA VALLES RAGILES, 40s + ERNESTO VILLANIA, nb
JV.2.2.2.5.1. AGNES RAGILES VILLANIA, 60s

JV.2.2.2.6. RUBEN VALLES RAGILES, 40s + BELLA CORTEZ, nb
JV.2.2.2.6.1. DEXTER CORTEZ RAGILES, 60s
JV.2.2.2.6.2. RIZZA CORTEZ RAGILES, 60s
JV.2.2.2.6.3. RUBEN CORTEZ RAGILES JR, 60s

JV.2.2.3. SOLEDAD CACHO VALLES, 10s + VICENTE ELEP, nb
JV.2.2.3.1. MARIA VALLES ELEP, 30s
JV.2.2.4. SIMPLICIO CACHO VALLES, 20s + GUADALUPE RAMOS, nb
JV.2.2.4.1. ALICIA RAMOS VALLES, 40s + ROLANDO GADIL, nb
JV.2.2.4.2. WENNIE RAMOS VALLES, 40s + MR. ORENDAIN, nb
JV.2.2.4.3. ANIANO RAMOS VALLES, 40s
JV.2.2.4.4. RAMIR RAMOS VALLES, 50s
JV.2.2.4.5. AMADA RAMOS VALLES, 50s
JV.2.2.4.6. MARILOU RAMOSVALLES, 50s

JV.2.2.5. PACIANIO CACHO VALLES, 20s + GLORIA DELA CRUZ, nb
JV.2.2.5.1. EMILIA DELACRUZ VALLES, 40s
JV.2.2.5.2. ANGEL DELACRUZ VALLES, 40s
JV.2.2.5.3. ELISA DELACRUZ VALLES, 40s
JV.2.2.5.4. AMADA DELACRUZ VALLES, 50s
JV.2.2.5.5. ANIANO DELACRUZ VALLES, 50s

JV.2.2.5.6. ARTURO DELACRUZ VALLES, 50s
JV.2.2.5.7. ERLINDA DELACRUZ VALLES, 60s
JV.2.2.5.8. NANING DELACRUZ VALLES, 60s

JV.2.2.6. FILIPINA CACHO VALLES, 20s + JESUS ZANTUA, nb
JV.2.2.6.1. VIRGINIA VALLES ZANTUA, 40s
JV.2.2.6.2. ROMELYN VALLES ZANTUA, 40s
JV.2.2.6.3. LINA VALLES ZANTUA, 40s
JV.2.2.6.4. RODEL VALLES ZANTUA, 50s
JV.2.2.6.5. ROMEO VALLES ZANTUA, 50s
JV.2.2.6.6. ARSENIA VALLES ZANTUA, 50s

JV.2.3. PETRA MAGANA VALLES, 1890s + PEDRO ABRERA, nb

JV.2.3.1. MODESTA ABRERA, 10s
JV.2.3.2. VALERIANO ABRERA, 10s
JV.2.3.3. JACINTO ABRERA, 10s
JV.2.3.4. RAFAEL ABRERA, 20s
JV.2.3.5. LUISA ABRERA, 20s

JV.2.4. SEVERINA MAGANA VALLES, 1900s + ANDRE RASCO, nb

JV.2.4.1. MARIA VALLES RASCO, 20s
JV.2.4.2. LEON VALLES RASCO, 20s
JV.2.4.3. PEDRO VALLES RASCO, 20s
JV.2.4.4. SOFIA VALLES RASCO, 20s

JV.3. TIBURCIA JAMITO VALLES, 1890s, rip
JV.4. PANTALEON JAMITO VALLES, 1890s + LUISA CAYNO, nb

JV.4.1. APOLINARIO CAYNO VALLES, 10s + ENGRACIA RALA, nb

Publisher - Tatay Jobo Elizes

JV.4.1.1. NATIVIDAD RALA VALLES, 30s
JV.4.1.2. AUGORIO RALA VALLES, 30s
JV.4.1.3. CESAR RALA VALLES, 30s
JV.4.1.4. DELFIN RALA VALLES, 30s
JV.4.1.5. RUBEN RALA VALLES, 40s
JV.4.1.6. JOSE RALA VALLES, 40s
JV.4.1.7. MARIO RALA VALLES, 40s

JV.4.2. INOCENCIA CAYNO VALLES, 10s + SEGUNDO PANCHO, nb

JV.4.2.1. DOLORES VALLES PANCHO, 30s + DOMINGO DIAZ, nb
JV.4.2.1.1. ADELINA PANCHO DIAZ, 50s + TOMAS STA.ANA, nb
JV.4.2.1.1.1. JOSEPH DIAZ STA.ANA, 70s
JV.4.2.1.1.2. NICANOR DIAZ STA.ANA, 70s
JV.4.2.1.1.3. NOEL DIAZ STA.ANA, 70S + LAILA, nb

JV.4.2.1.2. BENJAMIN PANCHO DIAZ, 50s + ANTONIA BRANDO, nb
JV.4.2.1.2.1. ARMIE BRANDO DIAZ, 70s + ROLANDO MANLANGIT, nb
JV.4.2.1.2.1.1. EDWIN DIAZ MANLANGIT, 90s
JV.4.2.1.2.1.2. JAY-JAY DIAZ MANLANGIT, 90s
JV.4.2.1.2.1.3. ODESSA DIAZ MANLANGIT, 90s
JV.4.2.1.2.1.4. IVY DIAZ MANLANGIT, 90s
JV.4.2.1.2.2. DOMINGO BRANDO DIAZ, 70s + HERMELINA COBALLES, nb
JV.4.2.1.2.2.1. DONNA GLAIZY COBALLES DIAZ, 90s
JV.4.2.1.2.2.2. BEN COBALLES DIAZ, 90s
JV.4.2.1.2.2.3. MARGIE COBALLES DIAZ, 90s

JV.4.2.1.3. GIL PANCHO DIAZ, 50s + MELICIA CERENO, nb
JV.4.2.1.3.1. ROMEO CERENO DIAZ, 70s + ARLYN ZENAROSA, nb
JV.4.2.1.3.1.1. ARDY ZENAROSA DIAZ, 90s
JV.4.2.1.3.1.2. AIMEE ZENAROSA DIAZ, 90s
JV.4.2.1.3.1.3. RONIEDYN ZENAROSA DIAZ, 90s
JV.4.2.1.3.1.4. ARIAN MAY ZENAROSA DIAZ, 90s

JV.4.2.1.3.2. ROE CERENO DIAZ, 70s + MARICHU APIN, nb
JV.4.2.1.3.2.1. MARIE JOY APIN DIAZ, 90s
JV.4.2.1.3.2.2. RIO MAY APIN DIAZ, 90s

JV.4.2.1.3.3. GILDA CERENO DIAZ, 70s + DANTE DE VERA, nb
JV.4.2.1.3.4. ROMY CERENO DIAZ, 70s + GRACE ZALETA, nb
JV.4.2.1.3.4.1. LYKA ZALETA DIAZ, 90s

JV.4.2.1.3.5. RUEL CERENO DIAZ, 80s
JV.4.2.1.3.6. REX CERENO DIAZ, 80s
JV.4.2.1.3.7. RHEA CERENO DIAZ, 80s

JV.4.2.2. GLICERIO VALLES PANCHO, 30s + SALVACION, nb
JV.4.2.2.1. FE SALVACION PANCHO, 50s
JV.4.2.2.2. DOLORES SALVACION PANCHO, 50s
JV.4.2.2.3. AUGUSTO SALVACION PANCHO, 50s
JV.4.2.2.4. EDWIN SALVACION PANCHO, 50s
JV.4.2.2.5. SALOME SALVACION PANCHO, 60s
JV.4.2.2.6. ROMEO SALVACION PANCHO, 60s
JV.4.2.2.7. GLICERIO SALVACION PANCHO JR, 60s
JV.4.2.2.8. ALVIN SALVACION PANCHO, 60s
JV.4.2.2.9. LINA SALVACION PANCHO, 70s
JV.4.2.2.10. MABINI SALVACION PANCHO, 70s

JV.4.2.3. PILAR VALLES PANCHO, 30s + JOSE ANG
JV.4.2.3.1. ONOFRE PANCHO ANG, 50s + BENILDA ABUYO, nb
JV.4.2.3.1.1. MA.TERESA ABUYO ANG, 70s + RONALD SIMEON, nb
JV.4.2.3.1.1.1. HENRY LOUIS ANG SIMEON, 90s
JV.4.2.3.1.1.2. PATRICK ANG SIMEON, 90s
JV.4.2.3.1.1.3. RONALD RYAN ANG SIMEON, 90s

JV.4.2.3.1.2. JEANINE ABUYO ANG, 70s + ROSERO GLIPO, nb
JV.4.2.3.1.2.1. JULIE ANN ANG GLIPO, 90S
JV.4.2.3.1.2.2. JACKIE LOU ANG GLIPO, 90s
JV.4.2.3.1.2.3. JOHN ROBERT ANG GLIPO, 90s

JV.4.2.3.2. DELFIN ABUYO ANG, 50s + MAGDALENA MAGANA, nb, W1 +
MERLINA EMBESTRO, nb, W2
JV.4.2.3.2.1. JULIO MAGANA ANG, 70s + FILOMENA ANGELES, nb
JV.4.2.3.2.1.1. CHRISTINA ANGELES ANG, 90s
JV.4.2.3.2.1.2. MA.GLORIA PAULA ANGELES ANG, 90s

Publisher - Tatay Jobo Elizes

JV.4.2.3.2.1.3. DAISY JANE ANGELES ANG, 90s
JV.4.2.3.2.1.4. DENNIS JOSE ANGELES ANG, 90s
JV.4.2.3.2.1.5. JOHN EMMANUEL ANGELES ANG, 2000s
JV.4.2.3.2.1.6. JOHN MICHAEL ANGELES ANG, 2000s
JV.4.2.3.2.1.7. ABIGAIL ANGELES ANG, 2000s
JV.4.2.3.2.1.8. JOHN PAULO ANGELES ANG, 2000s
JV.4.2.3.2.1.9. EMMA CONCEPCION ANGELES ANG, 2000s

JV.4.2.3.2.2. MA.ELENA MAGANA ANG, 70s + ROLANDO GONZALES, nb
JV.4.2.3.2.2.1. JANSON ANG GONZALES, 90s
JV.4.2.3.2.2.2. KYPER ANG GONZALES, 90s
JV.4.2.3.2.3. MEDEL EMBESTRO ANG, 70s + SHERYL FARLAN, nb
JV.4.2.3.2.3.1. JOHN MICHAEL FARLAN ANG, 90s

JV.4.2.3.2.4. CYNTHIA EMBESTRO ANG, 70s
JV.4.2.3.2.5. GEOFFREY EMBESTRO ANG, 70s
JV.4.2.3.2.6. DELFIN EMBESTRO ANG JR, 80s + LALLAINE MAGANA, nb
JV.4.2.3.2.6.1. LYN SUZETTE MAGANA ANG, 2000s
JV.4.2.3.2.7. RANDY EMBESTRO ANG, 80s
JV.4.2.3.2.8. JAN MEDELYN EMBESTRO ANG, 80s + RICKY
MARQUESAS, nb
JV.4.2.3.2.8.1. LATRELL ANG MARQUESAS, 2000s
JV.4.2.3.2.8.2. ALEJA SHYANNE ANG MARQUESAS, 2000s

JV.4.2.3.2.9. JOE GILSON EMBESTRO ANG, 90s
JV.4.2.3.2.10. JAN LAUREN EMBESTRO ANG, 90s
JV.4.2.3.2.11. JOHN LOUIE EMBESTRO ANG
JV.4.2.3.3. AMELIA PANCHO ANG, 40s + ZOSIMO MAPOL, nb
JV.4.2.3.3.1. EMILY ANG MAPOL, 60s
JV.4.2.3.3.2. AIMEE ROSE ANG MAPOL, 60s

JV.4.2.3.4. TRINIDAD PANCHO ANG, 40s + SIMEON DELA TORRE, nb
JV.4.2.3.4.1. SENEN ANG DELA TORRE, 60s + CHRISTINA CAPISTRANO,
nb
JV.4.2.3.4.1.1. JOHN MICHAEL CAPISTRANO DELA TORRE, 80s

JV.4.2.3.4.2. SUSAN ANG DELA TORRE, 60s + RONELO DIAZ, nb
JV.4.2.3.4.2.1. ROSALIE MAY DELA TORRE DIAZ, 80s

JV.4.2.3.4.2.2. ANNA DELATORRE DIAZ, 80s

JV.4.2.3.4.3. SONIA ANG DELA TORRE, 60s + DANTE BORJA, nb
JV.4.2.3.4.3.1. CHRISTOPHER JAY DELATORRE BORJA, 80s

JV.4.2.3.4.4. SHIELA ANG DELA TORRE, 60s
JV.4.2.3.4.5. SIMON ANG DELA TORRE, 70s
JV.4.2.3.4.6. SERNAN ANG DELA TORRE, 70s
JV.4.2.3.4.7. SHERWYN ANG DELA TORRE, 70s
JV.4.2.3.4.8. SHIEN ANG DELA TORRE, 70s

JV.4.2.3.5. VIRGINIA PANCHO ANG, 50s + PEDRO IGNACIO II, nb
JV.4.2.3.5.1. PEDRO ANG IGNACIO III, 70s + MARIA, nb
JV.4.2.3.5.2. PETERSON ANG IGNACIO, 70s
JV.4.2.3.5.3. NICHOLAS ANG IGNACIO, 70s

JV.4.2.3.6. ELENA PANCHO ANG, 50s
JV.4.2.3.7. ALICIA PANCHO ANG, 50s
JV.4.2.3.8. ARMANDO PANCHO ANG, 50s + ALICIA PANGO, nb
JV.4.2.3.8.1. JHONNA MARIEL PANGO ANG, 70s
JV.4.2.3.8.2. AMY GRACE PANGO ANG, 70s
JV.4.2.3.8.3. CHRISTINA PANGO ANG, 70s
JV.4.2.3.8.4. JOE MARI PANGO ANG, 70s

JV.4.2.3.9. EDGARDO PANCHO ANG, 60s + GILDA IBANA, nb
JV.4.2.3.9.1. JANICE IBANA ANG, 80s
JV.4.2.3.9.2. AL FRANCIS IBANA ANG, 80s
JV.4.2.3.9.3. JANE PATRICIA IBANA ANG, 80s
JV.4.2.3.9.4. JANUS BALTAZAR IBANA ANG, 80s
JV.4.2.3.9.5. JIOVANNI PAULO IBANA ANG, 90s
JV.4.2.3.9.6. PATRICIA JOYCE IBANA ANG, 90s
JV.4.2.3.9.7. MARY ROSE RAQUEL IBANA ANG, 90s

JV.4.2.3.10. SAMUEL PANCHO ANG, 60s + SUSAN GALLARDO, nb
JV.4.2.3.10.1. SANDRA GALLARDO ANG, 80s
JV.4.2.3.10.2. ROCHELLE GALLARDO ANG, 80s

JV.4.2.3.11. JOSE PANCHO ANG JR, 60s

JV.4.2.3.12. PATRICIO PANCHO ANG, 60s + FE QUIBRAL, nb
JV.4.2.3.12.1. JANE ROSE QUIBRAL ANG, 80s
JV.4.2.3.12.2. NIKKO ANGEL QUIBRAL ANG, 80s
JV.4.2.3.12.3. JOHN MICHAEL QUIBRAL ANG 80s
JV.4.2.3.12.4. MICHELLE QUIBRAL ANG, 90s
JV.4.2.3.12.5. PAULO JAY QUIBRAL ANG, 90s

JV.4.2.4. JUAN VALLES PANCHO, 20s, rip
JV.4.2.5. JOSE VALLES PANCHO, 30s + NOEMI BAMBA, nb
JV.4.2.5.1. EMERITA BAMBA PANCHO, 50s
JV.4.2.5.2. EMILIO BAMBA PANCHO, 50s
JV.4.2.5.3. EVA BAMBA PANCHO, 50s
JV.4.2.5.4. EDEN BAMBA PANCHO, 60s

JV.4.2.6. JESUS VALLES PANCHO, 30s + JUANA GARIDO, nb
JV.4.2.6.1. RAUL GARIDO PANCHO, 50s
JV.4.2.6.2. EVELYN GARIDO PANCHO, 50s
JV.4.2.6.3. EDWIN GARIDO PANCHO, 50s
JV.4.2.6.4. EDITA GARIDO PANCHO, 60s
JV.4.2.6.5. JESUS GARIDO PANCHO JR, 60s

JV.4.2.7. RICARDO PANCHO, 30s + JULIA ROLDAN, nb
JV.4.2.7.1. ROLANDO ROLDAN PANCHO, 50s + WIFE, nb
JV.4.2.7.1.1. JELYN PANCHO, 70s
JV.4.2.7.1.2. ROLDAN PANCHO, 70s
JV.4.2.7.1.3. RUEL PANCHO, 70s
JV.4.2.7.1.4. EXEQUIEL PANCHO, 80s
JV.4.2.7.1.5. CHRISTINA PANCHO, 80s
JV.4.2.7.1.6. DANIEL PANCHO, 80s

JV.4.2.7.2. RAMON ROLDAN PANCHO, 50s
JV.4.2.7.3. RAQUEL ROLDAN PANCHO, 50s + EDMUNDO BALLATA, nb
JV.4.2.7.3.1. VANESSA PANCHO BALLATA, 70s
JV.4.2.7.3.2. VLADIMIR PANCHO BALLATA, 70s
JV.4.2.7.3.3. IVY PANCHO BALLATA, 70s

JV.4.2.7.4. SEGUNDO ROLDAN PANCHO, 50s + ELENA CABANELA, nb
JV.4.2.7.4.1. MARIA ELENA CABANELA PANCHO, 70s

JV.4.2.7.5. ARELENE ROLDAN PANCHO, 60s
JV.4.2.7.6. JOHN ROLDAN PANCHO, 60s
JV.4.2.7.7. GINA ROLDAN PANCHO, 60s
JV.4.2.7.8. RICHARD ROLDAN PANCHO, 60s

JV.4.2.8. GUILLERMO VALLES PANCHO, 30s + LUCIA RADA, nb
JV.4.2.8.1. AURORA RADA PANCHO, 50s + NICOLAS MERCADO, nb
JV.4.2.8.1.1. ROMMEL PANCHO MERCADO, 70s

JV.4.2.8.2. ANITA RADA PANCHO, 50s + HENRY ABOLENCIA, nb
JV.4.2.8.2.1. KATRINA PANCHO ABOLENCIA, 70s
JV.4.2.8.2.2. JANRIE PANCHO ABOLENCIA, 70s
JV.4.2.8.2.3. RYNIE PANCHO ABOLENCIA, 70s
JV.4.2.8.2.4. PAULA LUZ PANCHO ABOLENCIA, 70s
JV.4.2.8.2.5. FRANCISCO PANCHO ABOLENCIA, 80s
JV.4.2.8.2.6. RYAN PANCHO ABOLENCIA, 80s

JV.4.2.8.3. ALBERTO RADA PANCHO, 50s + ANA RANA, nb
JV.4.2.8.3.1. ANTONETTE RANA PANCHO, 70s
JV.4.2.8.4. ARTURO RADA PANCHO, 50S + RHODORA SINA-ON, nb
JV.4.2.8.5. ALELIE RADA PANCHO, 60s
JV.4.2.8.6. ANALIZA RADA PANCHO, 60s + HUSBAND, nb
JV.4.2.8.6.1. CARL ANTHONY PANCHO-SURN.,80s+CARMELA LOU,nb
JV.4.2.8.6.2. ALYSA MARIE PANCHO-SURNAME, 80s
JV.4.2.8.6.3. KIMBERLY PANCHO-SURNAME, 80s
JV.4.2.8.7. ALEX RADA PANCHO, 60s + MARIFE MAGTIBAY, nb
JV.4.2.8.8. ARNEL RADA PANCHO, 60s

JV.5. CALIXTA JAMITO VALLES, 1880s + MANUEL RAMORES, nb

JV.5.1. SANTIAGO VALLES RAMORES, 1900s

JV.5.2. JUANA VALLES RAMORES, 1900s + ELIGIO TEODORO, nb

JV.5.3. HERMENEGILDO VALLES RAMORES, 1900s + GUILLERMA VALERIO, nb

JV.5.3.1. MARIA CANDELARIA VALERIO RAMORES, 20s
JV.5.3.2. VICTORIA VALERIO RAMORES, 20s + PANTALEON NIEVA, nb
JV.5.3.3. FAUSTA VALERIO RAMORES, 20s + JULIAN AMANTE, nb
JV.5.3.4. MODESTA VALERIO RAMORES, 20s
JV.5.3.5. DANIEL VALERIO RAMORES, 30s
JV.5.3.6. APOLONIA VALERIO RAMORES, 30s
JV.5.3.7. SEGUNDO VALERIO RAMORES, 30s + SIXTA RAFON, nb
JV.5.3.8. MARTA VALERIO RAMORES, 30s
JV.5.3.9. JUANA VALERIO RAMORES, 40s

JV.5.4. APOLINARIA VALLES RAMORES, 10s

JV.5.5. ESTEBAN VALLES RAMORES, 10s + JUANA PEDIR, nb, W1 + ELENA MAGANA, nb, W2

JV.5.5.1. BEATRIZ PEDIR RAMORES, 30s + EUGENIO MARIANO, nb
JV.5.5.2. ANTONINA PEDIR RAMORES, 30s
JV.5.5.3. AQUILINA PEDIR RAMORES, 30s
JV.5.5.4. TEOFILA PEDIR RAMORES, 40s + CORNELIO RAFON, nb
JV.5.5.5. SANTIAGO PEDIR RAMORES, 40s
JV.5.5.6. MARIA PEDIR RAMORES, 40s

JV.5.5.7. SALOMON MAGANA RAMORES, 60s

BRANCH NO. 4
SEVERINO JAMITO +
APOLINARIA BARILLA
(JB - JAMITO-BARILLA, 1850s)

Publisher - Tatay Jobo Elizes

JB.1. RUFINA BARILLA JAMITO, 1870s, Early rip

JB.2. MARIANO JAMITO, 1870s + FAUSTA PANOTES (NOT DELOS SANTOS)

JB.2.1. ILDEFONSO PANOTES JAMITO, 1890s-1997 + BARBARA OMOTO(nb), d.2004. *Ildefonso was U.S. Veteran.*

JB.2.1.1. DELIA OMOTO JAMITO, 1930S + HUSBAND BANTIGUE. Home: Loma Linda, CA. deliab12@hotmail.com

JB.2.1.1.1. JERSHON JAMITO BANTIGUE, 1960S + WIFE SURNAME. Home: CA, *jershb08@hotmail.com*

JB.2.1.2. FE OMOTO JAMITO, 1930S + HUSBAND SURNAME. Home: CA
JB.2.1.3. JENITA OMOTO JAMITO. 1930S + HUSBAND SURNAME. CA
JB.2.1.4. FLORENTINA OMOTO JAMITO, *Died in infancy*
(Message: Name: delia omoto jamito bantigue
Email: deliab12@hotmail.com Oct 10, 2008
Thank you once again for this website.....My father Ildefonso Panotes Jamito....married to Barbara Omoto....I think branch 4...Tatay passed away in 1997 and nanay passed away 2004...here in Loma Linda, California...It has been our great longing to meet any jamitos. My sisters Fe and Jenita....We miss them so much and would like to get aquainted with Jamitos......
Message: Name: DELIA JAMITO BANTIGUE
Email: deliab12@hotmail.com Oct 2, 2008
Wow...this was a pleasant surprise...when my son told me about this....I had tears my eyes....My father is Ildefonso Panotes Jamito
not Delos Santos and he married Barbara Omoto...We came to U.S. because my tatay was a U.S. Veteran.....My father came from Talisay Camarines Norte....I have a very sad, sad story of my father childhood as told to us ....I will be wriitting more ..Delia Jamito
Message: Name: Jershon J. Bantigue
Email: Jershb08@hotmail.com Sep 10, 2008
Ildefonso Delos Santos Jamito + Barbara Omoto had four daughters

Delia, Fe, Janita, and Florintina. Florintina however died in childbirth due to complications. I am the product of one of the four daughters, yet our names have seemed to be forgotten from the tree. Can anyone please guess what the J in my middle name is!?!?!? Plea)

JB.2.2. PORFIRIO PANOTES JAMITO, 1890s

JB.2.3. SEVERINO PANOTES JAMITO II, 1890s

JB.2.4. LOURDES PANOTES JAMITO, 1890s

JB.2.5. CESAR PANOTES JAMITO, 1900s

JB.3. VICTORIA BARILLA JAMITO, 1870s + DOMINGO ABRINA, nb

JB.3.1. DOMINGO JAMITO ABRINA JR, 1890s + JOSEFA MAGANA, nb

JB.3.1.1. NATIVIDAD MAGANA ABRINA, 10s + MANUEL MANLY, nb
(Manuel is brother of Teacher Mr. Manly and Nana Uling, parents of Monchie Manly Vargas, Jun Vargas wife,Jobo-Pub)

JB.3.1.1.1. JOSEFA (BABY) MANLY, 1953 + BERNARD L. SMITH, Home: *Fredricksburg, MD*
JB.3.1.1.1.1. EMMANUEL AARON SMITH (MANNY), 1982
JB.3.1.1.1.2. CECILIA ANN SMITH, 1992
(Message: About 2009: Hello Kuya TJ,
Si Tata Osing ay nasa Manila pirme.
He's in his 80's. Si Tio Flor and Tio Henry nasa Manila din. I haven't heard from Tio Henry, he is my favorite uncle. Si Ta Osing kasi sumpungin na. I will mention you to my uncles. Lolo Ingo passed away more than 20 years ago. He has a daughter from his 2nd marriage, who lives in New Jersey. She is related to the Zantua's, nieces of Mr Manly & Nana Uling, parents of Ate Monchie Vargas. Thank you for mentioning my uncles and lolo Ingo. Lolo Ingo makes the best matamis na kaob? I forgot the name.

Boy, we're really getting old, ha ha ha. Baby Manly. PS: I remember the Hollmann 3 beautiful girls from Manila. Maybe my sister Manuela will remember most of the names, she's good at finding relatives. My husband's name is Bernard L . Smith of Virginia Beach. My children are: Emmanuel Aaron Smith, 26 (Manny); Cecilia Ann Smith, 16 (Ceci), No grandchildren)

JB.3.1.1.2. MANUELA MANLY, b. + HUSBAND

JB.3.1.2. ERNESTO MAGANA ABRINA, 10s + ZOE EFA, nb
JB.3.1.2.1. MANUELA EFA ABRINA, 30s + PHILIP DALUPANG, nb
JB.3.1.2.1.1. PHIL MANUEL ABRINA DALUPANG, 50s
JB.3.2.2.1.2. PHILIP JASON ABRINA DALUPANG, 50s + SHIELA FAJARDO, nb
JB.3.2.2.1.2.1. PAOLO JOSHWA FAJARDO DALUPANG, 70s

JB.3.2.2.1.3. HARRY ABRINA DALUPANG, 50s + CRIS JENNIFER, nb
JB.3.2.2.1.3.1. HAYMON DALUPANG, 70s

JB.3.1.2.2. ELVIRA EFA ABRINA, 30s + SALVADOR JAVIER, nb
JB.3.1.2.3. DANILO EFA ABRINA, 30s

JB.3.1.2.4. ERNESTO EFA ABRINA JR, 30s + ELVIRA, nb
JB.3.1.2.4.1. JENELYN ELVIRA ABRINA, 50s
JB.3.1.2.4.2. JOCELYN ELVIRA ABRINA, 50s
JB.3.1.2.4.3. JONA ELVIRA ABRINA, 50s
JB.3.1.2.4.4. JOSEPHINE ELVIRA ABRINA, 50s
JB.3.1.2.4.5. ERWIN ELVIRA ABRINA, 60s
JB.3.1.2.4.6. ERVIN ELVIRA ABRINA, 60s
JB.3.1.2.4.7. ERSON ELVIRA ABRINA, 60s

JB.3.1.2.5. SYLVA EFA ABRINA, 40s + ROGELIO GREGORIO, nb
JB.3.1.2.5.1. ROWENA ABRINA GREGORIO, 60s
JB.3.1.2.5.2. ROSARIO ABRINA GREGORIO, 60s

JB.3.1.2.6. SYLMA EFA ABRINA, 40s + ROBERTO LABAN, nb
JB.3.1.2.6.1. ROBERT JOHN ABRINA LABAN, 60s
JB.3.1.2.6.2. ROBERTSON ABRINA LABAN, 60s

JB.3.1.2.7. ROBERTO EFA ABRINA, 40s + MARIA PARENTE, nb
JB.3.1.2.7.1. GIRLIE PARENTE ABRINA, 60s
JB.3.1.2.7.2. ROMART PARENTE ABRINA, 60s
JB.3.1.2.7.3. ROY VIN PARENTE ABRINA, 60s
JB.3.1.2.7.4. ROSE MARIE PARENTE ABRINA, 70s
JB.3.1.2.7.5. ROMA PARENTE ABRINA, 70s
JB.3.1.2.7.6. REN MARK PARENTE ABRINA, 70s

JB.3.1.2.8. MARIVIC EFA ABRINA, 40s
JB.3.1.2.9. HILBERT EFA ABRINA, 50s

JB.3.1.3. ROSAURO MAGANA ABRINA, 20s (Osing)
JB.3.1.4. MENARDO MAGANA ABRINA, 20s
JB.3.1.5. HENRY MAGANA ABRINA, 30s + WIFE H. *(Why Magana, when he uses Cuano as middle name?)*
JB.3.1.5.1. JAMES HENRY H. ABRINA, 1960S? james_henry_07@live.com
(Message: Name: James Henry H. Abrina
Email: james_henry_07@live.com
Date: Aug 27, 2008
Searching my name on the web really awed me with startling results...seeing a family tree I seem to belong with.
I was surprised to see my father's middle name (Magana here, but my father uses Cuaño; where did that come from?). I would be glad if somebody can enlighten me a bit 'bout that. My email ad is posted here (I guess) so please do contact me.
Definitely I will tell my father about this new discovery (Eureka...). It had been a very long time since my first and last visit to Talisay (I think that was the wake of "Ate Natty" as my father called her) so I am not really aware of anything posted here. Again I will ask my father about that.
Well again, it's nice to see something like this.
Thanks.)

JB.3.1.6. FLOR MAGANA ABRINA, 30s + GLORIA, nb
JB.3.1.6.1. ADONIS ABRINA, 50s
JB.3.1.6.2. SHIELA ABRINA, 50s
JB.3.1.7. ROMEO MAGANA ABRINA, 30s

Publisher - Tatay Jobo Elizes

JB.4. JUANA JAMITO, 1870s, rip

JB.5. RUPERTA BARILLA JAMITO, 1880s + FLORENTINO DIAZ, nb

JB.5.1. FILOMENA JAMITO DIAZ, 1890s + EUGENIO GUERRERO, nb

JB.5.1.1. ESTHER DIAZ GUERRERO, '14 + JOB ELIZES SR, nb
JB.5.1.1.1. SUSANA GUERRERO ELIZES, '33 + ARSENIO FERRER, nb
JB.5.1.1.2. JOB GUERRERO ELIZES JR, '34 + CORAZON RAMIREZ, nb,
Website: www.jobelizes.webs.com
Email: job_elizes@yahoo.com
JB.5.1.1.3. HILDA GUERRERO ELIZES, '39 + FEDERICO RAMIREZ, nb
JB.5.1.1.4. ROBERTO GUERRERO ELIZES, '43 + MERLIE CABALE, nb

JB.5.1.2. ELER DIAZ GUERRERO, '18 + ROSA LEGASPI, nb
JB.5.1.2.1. ELEANOR LEGASPI GUERRERO, '46 + ABEL ATIENZA, nb
JB.5.1.2.2. MINNA LEGASPI GUERRERO, '48 + JOSE MAGYAWE, nb
JB.5.1.2.3. CYNTHIA LEGASPI GUERRERO, '50 + GASPAR, nb, H1) +
ERNIE SAYERS, nb, H2
JB.5.1.2.4. EUGENE LEGASPI GUERRERO, '53, rip
JB.5.1.2.5. DAVID LEGASPI GUERRERO, '55 + MARY, nb

JB.5.1.3. NAOMI DIAZ GUERRERO, '20 + CHARLES HOLLMANN, nb
JB.5.1.3.1. CHIQUI GUERRERO HOLLMANN, '56 + PRANDY YULO, nb
JB.5.1.3.2. CHARLENE GUERRERO HOLLMANN, '58 + HUSBAND, nb
JB.5.1.3.3. MIMI GUERRERO HOLLMANN, '60

JB.5.1.4. ELISA DIAZ GUERRERO, '22 + MARIANO YOGORE JR. nb
JB.5.1.4.1. MARIANO GUERRERO YOGORE III, '46 + RITA PENAFLORIDA, nb

JB.5.1.4.2. EUGENE-ELER GUERRERO YOGORE, '48 + LYNNA CABONCE, nb, rip

JB.5.1.4.3. ELIZABETH LILLIAN GUERRERO YOGORE, '50 +CHESTER KATH, nb
JB.5.1.4.4. MARILYN PATRICIA GUERRERO YOGORE, '52 +GUY THOMPSON, nb
JB.5.1.4.5. MARY ELLEN GUERRERO YOGORE, '54 + EDWARD KIMMETH, nb
JB.5.1.4.6. JOHN PATRICK GUERRERO YOGORE, '65 + SHANNON, nb
JB.5.1.4.7. MICHELLE MONIQUE GUERRERO YOGORE, '70 +RUSTY JONES, nb

JB.5.1.5. SER DIAZ GUERRERO, '25 + ZENAIDA HERRERA, nb
JB.5.1.5.1. ALBERT HERRERA GUERRERO, '55 + ANITA, nb
JB.5.1.5.2. EMILY HERRERA GUERRERO, '57 + GERRY SICAT, nb
JB.5.1.5.3. NINA HERRERA GUERRERO, '60 + BONG MERCADO, nb
JB.5.1.5.4. SER HERRERA GUERRERO JR, '63 + MARIA ELIAZO, nb

JB.5.1.6. ARTE DIAZ GUERRERO, '27 + PRISCILLA ROXAS, nb
JB.5.1.6.1. JOCELYN ROXAS GUERRERO, '57 + DENNIS ACOP, nb
JB.5.1.6.2. MARINELLA ROXAS GUERRERO, '59 +RENE VALERIO, nb
JB.5.1.6.3. MARGARITA ROXAS GUERRERO, '61 + ARCY RADA, nb
JB.5.1.6.4. ARTURO ROXAS GUERRERO, '63 + CYNTHIA SERRANO, nb
JB.5.1.6.5. ARTEMIO ROXAS GUERRERO, '66 + GEORGIA, nb

JB.5.1.7. NORMA DIAZ GUERRERO, '30

JB.5.1.8. EUGENIO DIAZ GUERRERO JR, '34 + FEDERICA VILORIA, nb
JB.5.1.8.1. MARIFI VILORIA GUERRERO, 70s + PATRICK JAMES O'MALLEY, nb
JB.5.1.8.2. GENE GERRY VILORIA GUERRERO, 70s
JB.5.1.8.3. EURIC VILORIA GUERRERO, 70s
+ WIFE
JB.5.1.8.4. MELISSA FEDERICA VILORIA GUERRERO, 80s

JB.5.1.9. LULEX DIAZ GUERRERO, '36 + EDUARDO LICERIO, nb

JB.5.1.9.1. MARIE CLAIRE GUERRERO LICERIO, 70s + CARMELO SORIANO, nb

Publisher - Tatay Jobo Elizes

JB.5.1.9.2. EDUARDO GUERRERO LICERIO JR, 70s + JUDITH ESCALANTE, nb

JB.5.1.9.3. LAURIE JOY GUERRERO LICERIO, 70s + ELDON F. HART III, nb

JB.5.1.9.4. CHRISTINA GUERRERO LICERIO, 70s + MR. CRUZ, nb

JB.5.1.10. VENCER DIAZ GUERRERO, 30s + DIDI MISSION, nb

JB.5.1.10.1. MARIA THERESA MISSION GUERRERO, 70s + MICHAEL ALBA, nb

JB.5.1.10.2. MA.FELISA MISSION GUERRERO, 70s + REX RIBANO, nb-div.

JB.5.1.10.3. MA.FILOMENA MISSION GUERRERO, 70s + RICARDO CASTRO, nb

JB.5.1.10.4. VENCER KRYSTIAN MISSION GUERRERO, 80s

JB.5.1.10.5. JETHRO MISSION GUERRERO, 80s

JB.5.2. JUAN JAMITO DIAZ, 1900s, EARLY RIP-epidemic

JB.5.3. AGUSTIN JAMITO DIAZ, 1900S, EARLY RIP-epidemic

JB.5.4. ISIDORA JAMITO DIAZ, 1900s, EARLY RIP-epidemic

JB.5.5. CASIANO JAMITO DIAZ, 1900s, EARLY RIP-epidemic

JB.5.6. MARIA ROSARIO JAMITO DIAZ, 1900s, EARLY RIP-epidemic

JB.5.7. UNKNOWN JAMITO DIAZ, 1900s, EARLY RIP-epidemic

JB.5.8. UNKNOWN JAMITO DIAZ, 1900s, EARLY RIP-epidemic

JB.6. MARGARITA (ITA) BARILLA JAMITO , 1880s + RUPERTO MAGANA, nb

JB.6.1. ESPERIDION JAMITO MAGANA, 1900s + JULIA CAMPOMANES(nb)

JB.6.1.1. NIEVES CAMPOMANES MAGANA, 20s + PEDRO FREYRA(nb)

JB.6.1.1.1. FLERIDA MAGANA FREYRA, 40s

JB.6.1.1.2. PAQUITO MAGANA FREYRA, 40s

JB.6.1.1.3. LEA MAGANA FREYRA, 40s

JB.6.1.1.4. CORAZON MAGANA FREYRA, 40s

JB.6.1.1.5. RAMONA MAGANA FREYRA, 50s

JB.6.1.1.6. JOEL MAGANA FREYRA, 50s

JB.6.1.1.7. LILY MAGANA FREYRA, 50s

JB.6.1.1.8. LALA MAGANA FREYRA, 50s

JB.6.1.2. OFELIA CAMPOMANES MAGANA, 20s + JOSE AREVALO, nb
JB.6.1.2.1. EMMA MAGANA AREVALO, 40s + CRESTITO ARINES, nb
JB.6.1.2.1.1. CATHERINE AREVALO ARINES, 60s
JB.6.1.2.1.2. ERWIN AREVALO ARINES, 60s
JB.6.1.2.1.3. NATHANIEL AREVALO ARINES, 60s
JB.6.1.2.1.4. JESSAMAY AREVALO ARINES, 70s

JB.6.1.2.2. NILDA MAGANA AREVALO, 40s + OSCAR RAGASA, nb
JB.6.1.2.2.1. MARIA THERESA AREVALO RAGASA, 60s
JB.6.1.2.2.2. MARLON AREVALO RAGASA, 60s
JB.6.1.2.2.3. LOUIE AREVALO RAGASA, 60s
JB.6.1.2.2.4. REDENTOR AREVALO RAGASA, 70s
JB.6.1.2.2.5. RONALD AREVALO RAGASA, 70s

JB.6.1.2.3. ARLEN MAGANA AREVALO, 40s + NENITA RAFER, nb
JB.6.1.2.3.1. WILMA RAFER AREVALO, 60s
JB.6.1.2.3.2. MARICEL RAFER AREVALO, 60s
JB.6.1.2.3.3. ALLAN RAFER AREVALO, 60s
JB.6.1.2.3.4. ARNEL RAFER AREVALO, 70s
JB.6.1.2.3.5. ARNIE RAFER AREVALO, 70s
JB.6.1.2.3.6. UNKNOWN RAFER AREVALO, 70s
JB.6.1.2.3.7. UNKNOWN RAFER AREVALO, 80s

JB.6.1.2.4. HERMAN MAGANA AREVALO, 40s + ELENITA MAESA, nb
JB.6.1.2.5. IVAN MAGANA AREVALO, 50s + LORNA BARBOSA, nb
JB.6.1.2.5.1. MARVIN BARBOSA AREVALO, 70s
JB.6.1.2.5.2. JING BARBOSA AREVALO, 70s
JB.6.1.2.5.3. MICHELLE BARBOSA AREVALO, 70s
JB.6.1.2.5.4. REYNER BARBOSA AREVALO, 80s

JB.6.1.2.6. SAMUEL MAGANA AREVALO, 50s + CONNIE CAVINTE, nb
JB.6.1.2.6.1. CONSUELO CAVINTE AREVALO, 70s
JB.6.1.2.6.2. AILEN CAVINTE AREVALO, 70s
JB.61.2.6.3. JOMAR CAVINTE AREVALO, 70s
JB.6.1.2.7. MANUEL MAGANA AREVALO, 50s
JB.6.1.2.8. MYRNA MAGANA AREVALO, 50s + ERNESTO GETUYA, nb
JB.6.1.2.8.1. MICHAEL AREVALO GETUYA, 70s

Publisher - Tatay Jobo Elizes

JB.6.1.2.8.2. EMMANUEL AREVALO GETUYA, 70s
JB.6.1.2.8.3. ERWIN AREVALO GETUYA, 70s
JB.6.1.2.8.4. ERIC AREVALO GETUYA, 80s

JB.6.1.2.9. CLARO MAGANA AREVALO, 60s + DIONISIA CAMACHO, nb
JB.6.1.2.9.1. CARLO CAMACHO AREVALO, 80s
JB.6.1.2.9.2. BOLINGLING CAMACHO AREVALO, 80s
JB.6.1.1.9.3. CAMILO CAMACHO AREVALO, 80s

JB.6.1.2.10. ALBERTO MAGANA AREVALO, 60s + JOCELYN LABORDO, nb
JB.6.1.2.10.1. ALBERT LABORDO AREVALO, 80s

JB.6.1.2.11. JOSELITO MAGANA AREVALO, 60s + RAQUEL PARLAN, nb
JB.6.1.2.11.1. MARIA THERESA PARLAN AREVALO, 80s

JB.6.1.2.12. NENA MAGANA AREVALO, 70s + PEDRO VILLALUNA, nb
JB.6.1.2.12.1. ABEGAIL AREVALO VILLALUNA, 90s
JB.6.1.2.12.2. GINA AREVALO VILLALUNA, 90s
JB.6.1.2.12.3. JOHN PAUL AREVALO VILLALUNA, 90s
JB.6.1.2.12.4. JOMARI AREVALO VILLALUNA, 00s

JB.6.1.2.13. JAIME MAGANA AREVALO, 70s + CRISTINA ZANTUA, nb
JB.6.1.2.13.1. DIANA ALEA ZANTUA AREVALO, 90s
JB.6.1.2.13.2. JADE ANTHONY ZANTUA AREVALO, 90s

JB.6.1.3. RUPERTO CAMPOMANES MAGANA, 20s, RIP
JB.6.1.4. ADELINA CAMPOMANES MAGANA, 30s, RIP
JB.6.1.5. REMEDIOS CAMPOMANES MAGANA, 30s + PEDRO MURALLO, nb
JB.6.1.5.1. YONIE MAGANA MURALLO, 50s
JB.6.1.5.2. BONGBONG MAGANA MURALLO, 50s
JB.6.1.5.3. ELA MAGANA MURALLO, 50s

JB.6.2. SEVERO JAMITO MAGANA, 1900s + FELICISIMA DE PANIS, nb

Publisher - Tatay Jobo Elizes

JB.6.2.1. ZENAIDA DE PANIS MAGANA, 20s + CESAR CABANELA, nb
JB.6.2.1.1. ANALISA MAGANA CABANELA, 40s + MARLON GERONIO, nb
JB.6.2.1.1.1. MARIAN CABANELA GERONIO, 60s
JB.6.2.1.1.2. MARK ANTHONY CABANELA GERONIO, 60s

JB.6.2.2. ELISA DE PANIS MAGANA, 20s + CRESENTE BARRETO, nb
JB.6.2.2.1. RHODORA MAGANA BARRETO, 40s
JB.6.2.2.2. RHODERICK MAGANA BARRETO, 40s
JB.6.2.2.3. RONELO MAGANA BARRETO, 40s

JB.6.2.3. ADOLFO DE PANIS MAGANA, 20s + MELICIA DIMAS, nb
JB.6.2.4. SEVERO DE PANIS MAGANA JR, 20s + HELEN MOZADA, nb
JB.6.2.4.1. CARRIE MOZADA MAGANA, 40s + MAILA GONZALVO, nb
JB.6.2.4.1.1. GAIL MAYLARIE GONZALVO MAGANA, 60s
JB.6.2.4.1.2. GAYRE MYRIE GONZALVO MAGANA, 60s
JB.6.2.4.2. JENNIFER DE PANIS MAGANA, 40s + ROGELIO GARCIA, nb

JB.6.2.5. ERLINDA DE PANIS MAGANA, 30s + RAMON AGUIRRE, nb
JB.6.2.5.1. ARMANDO MAGANA AGUIRRE, 50s + MELANIE PASCUAL, nb
JB.6.2.5.1.1. MARK KEVIN PASCUAL AGUIRRE, 70s
JB.6.2.5.1.2. MARIA ANGELICA PASCUAL AGUIRRE, 70s

JB.6.2.5.2. MARY ANN MAGANA AGUIRRE, 50s + MERVIN OVERA, nb
JB.6.2.5.2.1. MARK ANGELO AGUIRRE OVERA, 70s
JB.6.2.5.3. RAMON MAGANA AGUIRRE, 50s

JB.6.2.6. RICARDO DE PANIS MAGANA, 30s + RECHILDA UYA, nb
JB.6.2.6.1. RIZALYN UYA MAGANA, 50s + HERMAN BONGATE, nb
JB.6.2.6.1.1. REYNAN MAGANA BONGATE, 70s
JB.6.2.6.1.2. RAFAEL MAGANA BONGATE, 70s
JB.6.2.6.2. DOLOROSA UYA MAGANA, 50s + VICTOR TROSO, nb
JB.6.2.6.2.1. FERONICA MAGANA TROSO, 70s
JB.6.2.6.3. SHERWIN UYA MAGANA, 50s
JB.6.2.6.4. RIZZANDRO UYA MAGANA, 60s
JB.6.2.7. OSCAR DE PANIS MAGANA, 40s + CELENIA VALEROS, nb
JB.6.2.7.1. IAN CESAR VALEROS MAGANA, 60s + JEAN CRUZ, nb
JB.6.2.7.1.1. CEEJAY CRUZ MAGANA, 80s

JB.6.2.7.2. DINAROSE VALEROS MAGANA, 60s

JB.6.2.8. MANUEL DE PANIS MAGANA, 40s + DOLORES PANONG, nb

JB.6.3. MAXIMA JAMITO MAGANA, 1900s + JUAN NAING, nb

JB.7. JULIAN BARILLA JAMITO, 1880s
+ OBALDA MAGANA, nb

JB.7.1. APOLONIA MAGANA JAMITO, 1900s + EMILIANO MASE, nb

JB.7.1.1. PAULA JAMITO MASE, 20s + CAYO UBANA, nb
JB.7.1.1.1. CAYO MASE UBANA JR, 40s + NILDA BAAY
JB.7.1.1.1.1. PRINCESS LYNETTE BAAY UBANA, 60s
JB.7.1.1.1.2. CAYO BAAY UBANA III, 60s

JB.7.1.1.2. GERONIMO MASE UBANA, 40s + REMEDIOS BASA, nb
JB.7.1.1.2.1. MARIA CECILIA BASA UBANA, 60s
JB.7.1.1.2.2. ALFREDO BASA UBANA, 60s
JB.7.1.1.2.3. GENEROSO BASA UBANA, 60s
JB.7.1.1.2.4. LANIE BASA UBANA, 60s
JB.7.1.1.2.5. MARU BASA UBANA, 70s
JB.7.1.1.2.6. LALA (SHIELA?) BASA UBANA, 70s

JB.7.1.1.3. GEORGE MASE UBANA, 40s + JOSEFINA, nb
JB.7.1.1.3.1. AMIELOU JOSEFINA UBANA, 60s
JB.7.1.1.3.2. ANALIZA JOSEFINA UBANA, 60s
JB.7.1.1.3.3. GEORGE JOSEFINA UBANA JR, 60s

JB.7.1.1.4. EDUARDO MASE UBANA, 40s + NORMA CRUCERO, nb
JB.7.1.1.4.1. EDEN CRUCERO UBANA, 60s + ANTHONY PENA, nb
JB.7.1.1.4.1.1. JOSE ANTHONY UBANA PENA, 80s
JB.7.1.1.5. AGELIO MASE UBANA, 50s + REBECCA JANE, nb
JB.7.1.1.5.1. NIDA JANE UBANA, 70s + FRANCISCO SIA, nb
JB.7.1.1.5.2. EMMA JANE UBANA, 70s + MR. JERSON, nb
JB.7.1.1.5.2.1. EMMAN UBANA JERSON, 90s

JB.7.1.1.5.3. ARNOLD JANE UBANA, 70s + MINDA ASUR, nb
JB.7.1.1.5.3.1. MARK ASUR UBANA, 90s
JB.7.1.1.5.3.2. LOVELY ASUR UBANA, 90s
JB.7.1.1.5.3.3. JAMAICA ASUR UBANA, 90s
JB.7.1.1.5.3.4. JOHN CARLO ASUR UBANA, 90s
JB.7.1.1.5.4. AGELIO JANE UBANA JR, 70s + ELIZABETH SOLIVEN, nb
JB.7.1.1.5.5. MARTE JANE UBANA, 80s + ROWENA RASCO, nb
JB.7.1.1.5.5.1. KRYSTAL JANE RASCO UBANA, 00s
JB.7.1.1.5.5.2. KRSITINE MARIE RASCO UBANA, 00s
JB.7.1.1.5.5.3. KRYSTOBAL RASCO UBANA, 00s
JB.7.1.1.5.5.4. ETRAN JANE RASCO UBANA, 00s

JB.7.1.1.5.6. CARMELITA JANE UBANA, 80s + RAUL DE JESUS, nb
JB.7.1.1.5.6.1. JETHRO UBANA DE JESUS, 00s
JB.7.1.1.5.6.2. IVAN UBANA DE JESUS, 00s

JB.7.1.1.5.7. REBECCA JANE UBANA, 80s
JB.7.1.1.5.8. ROBERT UBANA, 90s

JB.7.1.1.6. ERNESTO MASE UBANA, 50s + ERMELINDA GONZALES, nb
(W1)+ NELLIE BORROMEO, nb (W2)
JB.7.1.1.6.1. VICTOR GONZALES UBANA, 70s + GRACELYN PASCUAL,
nb
JB.7.1.1.6.1.1. JERICO VENCENT PASCUAL UBANA, 90s

JB.7.1.1.6.2. HECTOR GONZALES UBANA, 1967 + DEBBIE JALIMAO, nb
hgu_hector1967@yahoo.com
JB.7.1.1.6.2.1. HECTOR DAVE JALIMAO UBANA, 90s
JB.7.1.1.6.2.2. HARREN DANE JALIMAO UBANA, 90s
(Message:Name: hector g. ubana
Email: hgu_hector1967@yahoo.com
Date: Sep 24, 2007
My wife is Debbie Jalimao Ubana
My son: Hector Dave J. Ubana
Harren Dane J. Ubana)

JB.7.1.1.6.3. ARTHUR GONZALES UBANA, 70s + VILMA ECHAVEZ, nb

JB.7.1.1.6.3.1. CHRISTIAN NICOLE ECHAVEZ UBANA, 90s
JB.7.1.1.6.4. ALEX GONZALES UBANA, 80s
JB.7.1.1.6.5. ESTELA BORROMEO UBANA, 90s
JB.7.1.1.6.6. ESTELA MAIE BORROMEO UBANA, 90s

JB.7.1.1.7. NENITA MASE UBANA, 50s + RESTITUTO RAGOS, nb
JB.7.1.1.7.1. JUNIE UBANA RAGOS, 70s + ELMA SARION, nb
JB.7.1.1.7.1.1. NICOLE SARION RAGOS, 90s
JB.7.1.1.7.1.2. BIANCA SARION RAGOS, 90s
JB.7.1.1.7.2. ANJUNETTE UBANA RAGOS, 70s
JB.7.1.1.7.3. RESTY UBANA RAGOS, 70s + RUBY BUMATAY, nb
JB.7.1.1.7.3.1. RUSTY BUMATAY RAGOS, 90s
JB.7.1.1.7.4. JOHN UBANA RAGOS, 80s
JB.7.1.1.7.5. MARIE JUNETTE UBANA RAGOS, 80s

JB.7.1.2. FILOMENO JAMITO MASE, 20s + NARING ELLA, nb
JB.7.1.2.1. GILDA ELLA MASE, 40s
JB.7.1.2.2. BOY ELLA MASE, 40s
JB.7.1.2.3. NICK ELLA MASE, 40S

JB.7.1.3. MARIA JAMITO MASE, 20s + EUSEBIO JAMO, nb
JB.7.1.3.1. ROMEO MASE JAMO, 40s
JB.7.1.3.2. HECTOR MASE JAMO, 40s
JB.7.1.3.3. ROSALINDA MASE JAMO, 40s

JB.7.1.4. JOSE JAMITO MASE, 20s + JULIA ELLA, nb
JB.7.1.5. PILAR JAMITO MASE, 30s
JB.7.1.6. MARIO JAMITO MASE, 30s
JB.7.1.7. JESUS JAMITO MASE, 30s + NORMA VILLARENTE, nb
(Pls see further correction below)
(Message: email from Gemiano Mase, medz_916@yahoo.com dtd. 7/24/09
Good morning po.. Happy and excited to know na ganon pala talaga
kadami ang lahi nag Jamito Clan. By the way, I send this email to inform
you that I'am the youngest son of Jesus Jamito Mase. Apolonia
Jamito(JB.7.1) + Gemeniano Mase. Here is the list of the children of
Jesus Jamito Mase + Norma Villarente)

JB.7.1.7.1. EVELYN MASE + PRUDENCIO LIOP, nb

Publisher - Tatay Jobo Elizes

JB.7.1.7.1.1. DENVER MASE LIOP
JB.7.1.7.1.2. NINGNING MASE LIOP
JB.7.1.7.1.3. JUN JUN MASE LIOP

JB.7.1.7.2. NESTOR MASE + GLENDA SANTE, nb
JB.7.1.7.2.1. ZALDIVAR SANTE MASE
JB.7.1.7.2.2. SAMUEL SANTE MASE, rip
JB.7.1.7.2.3. EMMANETTE SANTE MASE
JB.7.1.7.2.4. YSMAEL SANTE MASE

JB.7.1.7.3. ROSARIO MASE + VAL GAMBALA, nb
JB.7.1.7.3.1. GIAN MASE GAMBALA
JB.7.1.7.3.2. KRISTLE MASE GAMBALA
JB.7.1.7.3.3. GIZELLE MASE GAMBALA

JB.7.1.7.4. LORNA MASE + EMMANUEL DELGADO, nb
JB.7.1.7.4.1. EMMANUEL MASE DELGADO JR, rip
JB.7.1.7.4.2. EMERITO MASE DELGADO
JB.7.1.7.4.3. EDUARDO MASE DELGADO
JB.7.1.7.4.4 ELENITA MASE DELGADO

JB.7.1.7.5. JESSIE MASE
JB.7.1.7.6. RAUL MASE + DORY IDOROT, nb
JB.7.1.7.6.1. KEN IDOROT MASE
JB.7.1.7.6.2. KENJIE BRENT IDOROT MASE
JB.7.1.7.6.3. KEITH BRYANT IDOROT MASE

JB.7.1.7.7. ALMA MASE + ROE PAJARILLO
JB.7.1.7.7.1. ALISA MASE PAJARILLO
JB.7.1.7.7.2. SOLO MASE PAJARILLO
JB.7.1.7.7.3. LOVEN MASE PAJARILLO
JB.7.1.7.8. GEMINIANO MASE + ELENITA MAGHIRANG, nb
JB.7.1.7.8.1. MA. LOURDES ELAINE MASE
(Thanks po... sana makatulong ito, mapasama sa updated list ng Jamito Clan. Medz Esam
medz_916@yahoo.com)
JB.7.1.8. LORETO JAMITO MASE, 30s
JB.7.1.9. FERNANDO JAMITO MASE, 40s

JB.8. CRESENCIANA BARILLA JAMITO, 1880s
+ PEDRO GASIS, nb

JB.8.1. VICENTA JAMITO GASIS, 1900s + MANUEL VARIN, nb

JB.8.1.1. ALEJANDRO GASIS VARIN, 10s + AURORA ABUYO(nb)
JB.8.1.1.1. PEDRO ABUYO VARIN, 30s + ROSITA, nb
JB.8.1.1.2. EDUARDO ABUYO VARIN, 30s + LUZ ZANTUA, nb
JB.8.1.1.2.1. ERICSON ZANTUA VARIN, 50s
JB.8.1.1.2.2. RICKY ZANTUA VARIN, 50s
JB.8.1.1.2.3. MA. VICTORIA ZANTUA VARIN, 50s
JB.8.1.1.2.4. EVANGELINE ZANTUA VARIN, 60s
JB.8.1.1.2.5. EMERSON ZANTUA VARIN, 60s
JB.8.1.1.2.6. TERESA ZANTUA VARIN, 60s
JB.8.1.1.2.7. EDONG ZANTUA VARIN, 60s

JB.8.1.2. JUAN GASIS VARIN, 10s RIP
JB.8.1.3. FAUSTINA GASIS VARIN, 10s + LEON COOTAUCO, nb
JB.8.1.3.1. ELENA VARIN COOTAUCO, 30s + RODOLFO GARCIA, nb
JB.8.1.3.1.1. ARNEL COOTAUCO GARCIA, 50s
JB.8.1.3.1.2. ELMER COOTAUCO GARCIA, 50s
JB.8.1.3.1.3. ANA ROSANA COOTAUCO GARCIA, 60s
JB.8.1.3.1.4. AILEEN COOTAUCO GARCIA, 60s
JB.8.1.3.1.5. VICENTE COOTAUCO GARCIA, 60s
JB.8.1.3.1.6. IRMA COOTAUCO GARCIA, 60s

JB.8.1.3.2. JOSE VARIN COOTAUCO, 30s RIP
JB.8.1.3.3. CONSORCIA VARIN COOTAUCO, 30s
JB.8.1.3.4. NENITA VARIN COOTAUCO, 30s + ABSALOM ZENAROSA, nb
JB.8.1.3.4.1. ZANDRO JOHN COOTAUCO ZENAROSA, 50s
JB.8.1.3.4.2. FATIMA COOTAUCO ZENAROSA, 60s

JB.8.1.3.5. SOLEDDAD VARIN COOTAUCO, 40s + JOVENCIO YAP, nb
JB.8.1.3.5.1. MA. CHRISTINA COOTAUCO YAP, 60s
JB.8.1.3.5.2. JERRY COOTAUCO YAP, 60s
JB.8.1.3.5.3. JUDE ESTELITO COOTAUCO YAP, 60s

Publisher - Tatay Jobo Elizes

JB.8.1.3.6. ALFREDO VARIN COOTAUCO, 40s + ROSALINDA ROBLES, nb
JB.8.1.3.6.1. ALFREDO ROBLES COOTAUOCO JR, 60s
JB.8.1.3.6.2. STACEY ROBLES COOTAUCO, 60s

JB.8.1.3.7. JAIME VARIN COOTAUCO, 40s + ARACELI VILLA, nb
JB.8.1.3.7.1. ANABELLA VILLA COOTAUCO, 60s
JB.8.1.3.7.2. JAIME VILLA COOTAUCO JR, 60s
JB.8.1.3.7.3. MARCOS VILLA COOTAUCO, 60s
JB.8.1.3.7.4. NOEL VILLA COOTAUCO, 70s
JB.8.1.3.7.5. BRENDA VILLA COOTAUCO, 70s
JB.8.1.3.7.6. IMEE VILLA COOTAUCO, 70s
JB.8.1.3.7.7. ROLDA VILLA COOTAUCO, 70s
JB.8.1.3.7.8. ALVIN VILLA COOTAUCO, 80s
JB.8.1.3.7.9. JULIUS VILLA COOTAUCO, 80s
JB.8.1.3.7.10. RACHEL VILLA COOTAUCO, 80s

JB.8.1.3.8. EFREN VARIN COOTUACO, 40s + NORMA MARCILLA,nb (W1) + EMMA QUIOZON, nb (W2)
JB.8.1.3.8.1. EVELYN MARCILLA COOTUACO, 60s + (Not Wed) MARIO MENDOZA, nb, 60s
JB.8.1.3.8.1.1. NORMAN BOB COOTAUCO (MENDOZA),
(bob_bryar012yahoo.com, the one who sent this message, dtd.8/1/10)

JB.8.1.3.8.1.2. EVELYN COOTAUCO (MENDOZA), 60s + ROLITO MANZANO, nb
JB.8.1.3.8.1.3. WINSTON COOTAUCO (MENDOZA)
JB.8.1.3.8.1.4. JAIRO COOTAUCO (MENDOZA)

(Norman Email dtd. 8/1/10. . ."Kasali po kami, apo po ako ni EFREN VARIN COOTUACO, 40s + NORMA MARCILLA,nb.
Anak po ako ni Evelyn Marcilla Cootauco, 60's + Mario Mendoza, RIP, 60's =...Norman Cootauco+ at may kapatid pa ako on mother side.
Evelyn Marcilla Cootauco, 60's + Rolito Manzano, 60's,+...Winston Cootauco +...Jairo Cootauco

Publisher - Tatay Jobo Elizes

At anak po ni RICO MARCILLA COOTAUCO, 70's + Jocelyn Eco(nb) =
...Kristine Joy Eco Cootauco +...Kristian Paul Eco Cootauco

At anak po ni JB.8.1.4.10. DOLORES VARIN RAMORES, 60s + ENRIQUE
CABRIANO(nb) =
ay si Mikka Angela Cabriana, sunod po siya kay Mikko.

Note: I, Norman, Winston and Jairo weren't able to use our father's
Mendoza surname because it was stated by the law that we use our
mother's Cootauco surname but we should not use our mother's middle
initial if parents are not married, and Cootauco is our official surname
base on the approval of National Statistics Office. Thank you and hope
we'll be added soon. God Bless! We are honored to be in the Jamito
Generation. You're Very good.)

JB.8.1.3.8.2. FERDINAND MARCILLA COOTAUCO, 60s
JB.8.1.3.8.3. EFREN MARCILLA COOTAUCO JR, 60s
JB.8.1.3.8.4. RICO MARCILLA COOTAUCO, 70s + EVELYN ECO, nb
JB.8.1.3.8.4.1. KRISTINE JOY ECO COOTAUCO
JB.8.1.3.8.4.2. KRISTIAN PAUL ECO COOTAUCO

JB.8.1.3.8.5. JOEL QUIOZON COOTAUCO, 70s, *joel_cootauco@yaho.com*
+ JULIET OLIVER CANO, nb. JOEL WORK-PNP
JB.8.1.3.8.5.1. ANGELO DANIEL CANO COOTAUCO
JB.8.1.3.8.5.2. FRINZES HEART CANO COO.
JB.8.1.3.8.5.3. VANIE JILL CANO COOTAUCO

(Message: <joel_cootauco@yahoo.com>
Subject: clarification
To: job_elizes@yahoo.com
Date: Thursday, April 1, 2010, 10:46 AM
Good day!!!
 I am very much thankful for what you have done about our clan. I was
so amazed... how did you do that, tracing members of family which for
me I think I couldn't remember for some of them were already gone away.
Well any way, I just want to clarify that my middle name was Quiozon and
not Marcilla. My father got two relationship when he was still alive which
was not indicated in that family three. But then, however I think its too

late to change nor to update that... again thank you and God Bless to the entire family of us...Joel

----

Hello Tatay Jobo!!! (dtd. April 4,2010)
My mother was Emma G. Quiozon but they were not able to got married with my father Efren. Actually we are 5 of their children and I was the oldest one, next to me was Alma Quiozon, followed by Erica Q. Cootauco and our youngest twin sister Ma. Mara Quiozon and Ma. Clara Quiozon. At the age of 19 I got married with Juliet Oliver Cano and was gifted with 3 Children namely Angelo Janiel, Frinzes Heart and Vanie Jill. I'm working in the PNP with temporary status at present. My mother and my youngest twin sisters were all living at Dasmariñas Cavite, they move on 3 years before the death of our father. Alma and Erica were working as singers in Korea. With regards to Aunt Elen, I am sorry but I guest its good to ask other relatives of ours, I don't have any news from them. Joel)

JB.8.1.3.8.6. ALMA QUIOZON COOTAUCO, 70s, Singer, Korea
JB.8.1.3.8.7. ERICA QUIOZON COOTAUCO, 70s, Singer, Korea
JB.8.1.3.8.8. MA. MARA QUIOZON COOTAUCO, 80s, twin sister
JB.8.1.3.8.9. MA. CLARA QUIOZON COOTAUCO, 80s, twin sister

JB.8.1.3.9. LYDIA VARIN COOTAUCO, 50s + VIRGILIO TALAY, nb
JB.8.1.3.9.1. GIL COOTAUCO TALAY, 70s
JB.8.1.3.9.2. LEO COOTAUCO TALAY, 70s
JB.8.1.3.9.3. LIZA COOTAUCO TALAY, 70s

JB.8.1.3.10. VIRGINIA VARIN COOTAUCO, 50s + MANUEL ESTRADA, nb
JB.8.1.3.10.1. MAVELYN COOTAUCO ESTRADA, 70s
JB.8.1.3.10.2. MELANYE COOTAUCO ESTRADA, 70s

JB.8.1.3.11. ARMANDO VARIN COOTAUCO, 50s + THELMA QUIJANO, nb, Mississauga, Ontario
JB.8.1.3.11.1. ALMA QUIJANO COOTAUCO, 80s, acsphinx@hotmail.com, Burlington, Ontario, Proj Mgr, Hospital
(Message: 7/30/2010 from Alma
Hi Jobo,   Wow that's wonderful and thank you for all the work you have done, as lineage is a difficult to map out!!
My Parents live in Mississauga, Ontario. I live in Burlington, Ontario. I

Publisher - Tatay Jobo Elizes

was born in the 80's. My Brothers name is Jeffrey and he was also born in the 80s. I work as a Project Manager in a hospital. God Bless. ~~Alma~~

Alma Cootauco <acsphinx@hotmail.com> wrote: Hi, I was just wondering how you were able to collect all this information. Our family is in here and was just interesting to come across this. Alma Cootauco)

JB.8.1.3.11.2. ARMANDO (JEFFREY) QUIJANO COOTAUCO JR, 80s

JB.8.1.4. FILOMENA GASIS VARIN, 20s + JOSE RAMORES, nb
JB.8.1.4.1. RUBEN VARIN RAMORES, 40s + PATRICIA BARBOSA, nb
JB.8.1.4.1.1. NAIREEN BARBOSA RAMORES, 60s
JB.8.1.4.1.2. AELEEN BARBOSA RAMORES, 60s

JB.8.1.4.2. DANILO VARIN RAMORES, 40s + LOLITA BAUTISTA, nb
JB.8.1.4.2.1. DIANA BAUTISTA RAMORES, 60s
JB.8.1.4.2.2. DANIEL JOSE BAUTISTA RAMORES, 60s
JB.8.1.4.2.3. DOUGLAS BAUTISTA RAMORES, 60s

JB.8.1.4.3. NILDA VARIN RAMORES, 40s + JERRY DIN, nb
JB.8.1.4.3.1. GERALD RAMORES DIN, 60s
JB.8.1.4.3.2. LIZEL RAMORES DIN, 60s

JB.8.1.4.4. JOVITA VARIN RAMORES, 40s + CRISPIN RECONDO, nb
JB.8.1.4.4.1. JURICK RAMORES RECONDO, 60s
JB.8.1.4.4.2. JANELLE RAMORES RECONDO, 60s
JB.8.1.4.5. ALEX VARIN RAMORES, 50s + DOLORES ABEJERO, nb
JB.8.1.4.5.1. RONALD ABEJERO RAMORES, 70s
JB.8.1.4.5.2. RONALYN ABEJERO RAMORES, 70s + MR. ROJAS, nb
(Message: Email: ronalyn.rojas@gmail.com
Date: Fri Jan 9 17:06:43 GMT-12:00 2009
Hello! i'm so amazed when i browse this site, it was my husband who told me about this, ang galing nman po ninyo, na-trace nyo buong henerasyon ng Jamito, wow!
I'm from the family of JB.8. CRESENCIANA BARILLA JAMITO & PEDRO GASIS, grandparents ko po sina JB.8.1.4. FILOMENA GASIS VARIN & JOSE RAMORES, parents ko po sina ALEX VARIN RAMORES &

DOLORES VARGAS ABEJERO (nb)

May Additional info & correction lang po sana sa entry ng family namin, send ko po s e-mail nyo, thanks! More Power & GOD bless)
JB.8.1.4.5.3. ROCHELLE ABEJERO RAMORES, 70s
JB.8.1.4.5.4. ALEX ABEJERO RAMORES JR, 70s

JB.8.1.4.6. JOCELYN VARIN RAMORES, 50s + GERARDO ECO, nb
JB.8.1.4.6.1. JELYN RAMORES ECO, 70s
JB.8.1.4.6.2. JOLAN RAMORES ECO, 70s

JB.8.1.4.7. ROY VARIN RAMORES, 50s + FLERIDA ICATLO, nb
JB.8.1.4.7.1. JEFFREY ICATLO RAMORES, 70s
JB.8.1.4.7.2. JERYL ICATLO RAMORES, 70s
JB.8.1.4.7.3. MARIFLER ICATLO RAMORES, 70s

JB.8.1.4.8. EDEN VARIN RAMORES, 50s + DAMASO PAQUEO, nb
JB.8.1.4.8.1. ADAM JONAS RAMORES PAQUEO, 70s

JB.8.1.4.9. ALELI VARIN RAMORES, 60s + SANTIAGO BOTARDO JR, nb
JB.8.1.4.9.1. ANALIZA RAMORES BOTARDO, 80s
JB.8.1.4.9.2. JULIE ANN RAMORES BOTARDO, 80s
JB.8.1.4.9.3. ALJAN RAMORES BOTARDO, 80s

JB.8.1.4.10. DOLORES VARIN RAMORES, 60s + ENRIQUE CABRIANO, nb
JB.8.1.4.10.1. MIKKO RAMORES CABRIANO, 80s
JB.8.1.4.10.2. MIKKA ANGEL CABRIANO, 80s

JB.8.1.5. LEON GASIS VARIN, 20s + ASUNCION DELA CRUZ, nb
JB.8.1.5.1. EMERITA DELACRUZ VARIN, 40s + MARCIAL MARCELO, nb
JB.8.1.5.1.1. JACKIE VARIN MARCELO, 60s
JB.8.1.5.1.2. JOHN PAUL VARIN MARCELO, 60s
JB.8.1.5.1.3. JOYCE VARIN MARCELO, 60s

JB.8.1.5.2. RENATO DELACRUZ VARIN, 40s + SHIRLEY ABELLO, nb
JB.8.1.5.2.1. SHIENNA MAY ABELLO VARIN, 60s
JB.8.1.5.2.2. REYNALYN ABELLO VARIN, 60s

JB.8.1.5.3. VICTOR DELACRUZ VARIN, 40s + JESSICA YAO, nb
JB.8.1.5.3.1. LIESEL YAO VARIN, 60s
JB.8.1.5.3.2. VINCENT YAO VARIN, 60s

JB.8.1.5.4. ARNULFO DELACRUZ VARIN, 40s + MARILYN, nb
JB.8.1.5.4.1. RYAN MARILYN VARIN, 60s
JB.8.1.5.4.2. MARLON MARILYN VARIN, 60s
JB.8.1.5.4.3. JAKE MARILYN VARIN, 60s
JB.8.1.5.4.4. TONTON MARILYN VARIN, 70s
JB.8.1.5.4.5. NOYNOY MARILYN VARIN, 70s

JB.8.1.5.5. LANIE DELACRUZ VARIN, 50s + SAMIEL LOU, nb
JB.8.1.5.5.1. LEANDRO VARIN LOU, 70s
JB.8.1.5.5.2. RAYMOND VARIN LOU, 70s
JB.8.1.5.5.3. WILSON VARIN LOU, 70s
JB.8.1.5.5.4. ERICSON VARIN LOU, 70s

JB.8.1.5.6. ERLINDA DELACRUZ VARIN, 50s + JESUS TIMBALOPEZ, nb
JB.8.1.5.6.1. PAOLO VARIN TIMBALOPEZ, 70s
JB.8.1.5.6.2. LEOPOLDO VARIN TIMBALOPEZ, 70s
JB.8.1.5.7. ELSIE DELACRUZ VARIN, 50s + MARIE SARABILLO, nb
JB.8.1.5.7.1. MARA SARABILLO VARIN, 70s
JB.8.1.5.7.2. JAKE SARABILLO VARIN, 70s

JB.8.1.5.8. MERLE DELACRUZ VARIN, 50s + RAUL CARINO, nb
JB.8.1.5.8.1. MARIEL VARIN CARINO, 70s
JB.8.1.5.8.2. RAMIL VARIN CARINO, 70s
JB.8.1.5.8.3. MARJORIE VARIN CARINO, 70s

JB.8.1.5.9. MANUEL DELACRUZ JULIAN VARIN, 60s+MARILYN DIAZ, nb
JB.8.1.5.9.1. CHRISTIAN DIAZ VARIN, 80s
JB.8.1.5.9.2. CHARLENE DIAZ VARIN, 80s
JB.8.1.5.9.3. JARLYN DIAZ VARIN, 80s

JB.8.1.5.10. DANTE DELACRUZ VARIN, 60s + MARIA LESLIE, nb
JB.8.1.5.10.1. DANCEL ANN LESLIE VARIN, 80s
JB.8.1.5.10.2. DANIELA ANN LESLIE VARIN, 80s

Publisher - Tatay Jobo Elizes

JB.8.1.5.11. EDWIN DELACRUZ VARIN, 60s + JUDY ABELLO, nb
JB.8.1.5.11.1. NICOLE ANNE ABELLO VARIN, 80s

JB.8.1.6. ROSITA GASIS VARIN, 20s + ALFONSO MARCELO, nb

JB.8.1.7. RAFAEL GASIS VARIN, 20s + LARINA MARAS, nb

JB.8.1.7.1. MARTE MARAS VARIN, 40s + IMELDA GABUYA, nb
JB.8.1.7.1.1. JASON GABUYA VARIN, 60s

JB.8.1.7.2. DELSA MARAS VARIN, 40s + ELIANO DELOS SANTOS, nb
JB.8.1.7.2.1. KAREN VARIN DELOS SANTOS, 60s
JB.8.1.7.2.2. ERIC VARIN DELOS SANTOS, 60s
JB.8.1.7.2.3. BARBIE VARIN DELOS SANTOS, 60s
JB.8.1.7.2.4. DON VARIN DELOS SANTOS, 70s

JB.8.1.7.3. MARISSA MARAS VARIN, 40s + LEOPOLDO QUIRUBIN, nb
JB.8.1.7.3.1. JAY VARIN QUIRUBIN, 60s
JB.8.1.7.3.2. MARLO VARIN QUIRUBIN, 60s
JB.8.1.7.3.3. ANALYN VARIN QUIRUBIN, 60s
JB.8.1.7.3.4. LEOPOLDO VARIN QUIRUBIN JR, 70s

JB.8.1.7.4. MELISA MARAS VARIN, 40s + ROD DE LEON, nb
JB.8.1.7.4.1. ROSSEL VARIN DE LEON, 60s
JB.8.1.7.4.2. RUBY VARIN DE LEON, 60s
JB.8.1.7.4.3. ROY DE LEON, 60s

JB.8.1.7.5. SUSAN MARAS VARIN, 50s + REY TRAPANE, nb
JB.8.1.7.5.1. ROMEL VARIN TRAPANE, 70s
JB.8.1.7.5.2. RUEL VARIN TRAPANE, 70s
JB.8.1.7.5.3. RAYMOND VARIN TRAPANE, 70s

JB.8.1.7.6. LORENA MARAS VARIN, 50s + ROMULO MIGUEL, nb
JB.8.1.7.6.1. MICHAELA ALEXANDRIA VARIN MIGUEL, 70s

JB.8.1.7.7. RAFAEL MARAS VARIN JR, 50s, *rafael_varin@yahoo.com*

JB.8.1.7.8. ROWENA MARAS VARIN, 50s
JB.8.1.7.9. WILMA MARAS VARIN, 60s + GREGORIO FRIVALDO, nb
JB.8.1.7.9.1. RALPH CESAR VARIN FRIVALDO, 80s

JB.8.1.7.9.2. JOAN GABRIELA VARIN FRIVALDO, 80s

JB.8.1.7.10. EDITA MARAS VARIN, 60s + GLENMORE SAVILLA, nb
JB.8.1.7.10.1. GELLYN VARIN SAVILLA, 80s
JB.8.1.7.10.2. EDISON CANDIDO VARIN SAVILLA, 80s
JB.8.1.7.10.3. DANIEL VARIN SAVILLA, 80s
JB.8.1.7.10.4. BIANCA LARINA VARIN SAVILLA, 90s

JB.8.2. TEODORO JAMITO GASIS, 1900s + CARMEN CUBINAR, nb

JB.8.2.1. PORFIRIO CUBINAR GASIS, 20s + VALENTINA BACOLOR, nb
JB.8.2.1.1. FERNANDO BACOLOR GASIS, 40s + LITA, nb
JB.8.2.1.1.1. JECK JECK LITA GASIS, 60s
JB.8.2.1.1.2. JOSA LITA GASIS, 60s

JB.8.2.1.2. METRANO BACOLOR GASIS, 40s + ROSITA, nb
JB.8.2.1.2.1. MARITES ROSITA GASIS, 60s
JB.8.2.1.3. SALVADOR BACOLOR GASIS, 40s + VIRGINIA RICAFORT, nb
JB.8.2.1.4. ALFREDO BACOLOR GASIS, 40s + ELISA SALVADOR, nb
JB.8.2.1.4.1. RUEL SALVADOR GASIS, 60s + GENITA, nb
JB.8.2.1.4.2. ROLANDO SALVADOR GASIS, 60s

JB.8.2.1.5. GLORIA BACOLOR GASIS, 50s + WILFREDO BUENO, nb
JB.8.2.1.5.1. JONNA GASIS BUENO, 70s
JB.8.2.1.5.2. TERESA GASIS BUENO, 70s
JB.8.2.1.5.3. CHIQUI GASID BUENO, 70s

JB.8.2.1.6. ANTONIO BACOLOR GASIS, 50s + IMELDA CALLO, nb
JB.8.2.1.6.1. JORGE CALLO GASIS, 70s
JB.8.2.1.6.2. JONAS CALLO GASIS, 70s
JB.8.2.1.6.3. JARWYN CALLO GASIS, 70s
JB.8.2.1.6.4. GENELYN CALLO GASIS, 80s

JB.8.2.1.7. ANGEL BACOLOR GASIS, 50s + DELMA EFONDO, nb
JB.8.2.1.7.1. WILBERT EFONDO GASIS, 70s
JB.8.2.1.7.2. ALVIN EFONDO GASIS, 70s
JB.8.2.1.7.3. ARLEEN EFONDO GASIS, 70s
JB.8.2.1.7.4. ANGELO EFONDO GASIS, 80s

JB.8.2.1.8. FRANCIA BACOLOR GASIS, 60s + RICARDO VICTA, nb
JB.8.2.1.8.1. MARY ANNE GASIS VICTA, 80s
JB.8.2.1.8.2. NONONG GASIS VICTA, 80s
JB.8.2.1.8.3. KENT GASIS VICTA, 80s

JB.8.2.1.9. PORFIRIO BACOLOR GASIS JR, 60s + RIZALINA, nb
JB.8.2.1.9.1. CHRISTOPHER RIZALINA GASIS, 80s
JB.8.2.1.9.2. JOY RIZALINA GASIS, 80s

JB.8.2.2. FLORA CUBINAR GASIS, 20s + EDUARDO CUANO, nb
JB.8.2.2.1. CONRADO GASIS CUANO, 40s + NORMA ESPELETA, nb
JB.8.2.2.1.1. ERWIN ESPELETA CUANO, 60s
JB.8.2.2.1.2. HEIDI ESPELETA CUANO, 60s
JB.8.2.2.1.3. ALVIN ESPELETA CUANO, 60s
JB.8.2.2.1.4. MARICHU ESPELETA CUANO, 70s
JB.8.2.2.1.5. GLENN ESPELETA CUANO, 70s
JB.8.2.2.1.6. MELVIN ESPELETA CUANO, 70s

JB.8.2.2.2. HECTOR GASIS CUANO, 40s + LYDIA CANO, nb
JB.8.2.2.2.1. JUTJUT CANO CUANO, 60s
JB.8.2.2.2.2. CARLO CANO CUANO, 60s
JB.8.2.2.2.3. KATHY CANO CUANO, 60s
JB.8.2.2.2.4. DONNA CANO CUANO, 70s
JB.8.2.2.2.5. ANNA CANO CUANO, 70s

JB.8.2.2.3. GILDA CANO CUANO, 40s + HUSBAND, nb
JB.8.2.2.3.1. MARICEL CUANO-SURNAME, 60S

JB.8.2.2.4. ADOLFO CANO CUANO, 40s + NATIVIDAD SANCHEZ, nb
JB.8.2.2.4.1. MICHAEL SANCHEZ CUANO, 60s

JB.8.2.2.4.2. CHRISTOPHER SANCHEZ CUANO, 60s

Publisher - Tatay Jobo Elizes

JB.8.2.2.4.3. PAMELA SANCHEZ CUANO, 60s

JB.8.2.2.5. EDUARDO CANO CUANO JR, 50s + JOY, nb
JB.8.2.2.5.1. DENNIS JOY CUANO, 70s
JB.8.2.2.5.2. FRANCIS JOY CUANO, 70s

JB.8.2.2.6. LUISABEL CANO CUANO, 50s + RICHARD MAKALINTAL, nb
JB.8.2.2.6.1. HANNAHBEL CUANO MAKALINTAL, 70s

JB.8.2.2.7. NEMIA CANO CUANO, 50s + ODDIE CARAMOAN, nb
JB.8.2.2.7.1. JOSHWA CUANO CARAMOAN, 70s

JB.8.2.2.8. MANFRED CANO CUANO, 50s + SUSAN HERRERA, nb
JB.8.2.2.8.1. ANGELYN MAY HERRERA CUANO, 70s
JB.8.1.2.8.2. MARK VINCENT HERRERA CUANO, 70s

JB.8.2.2.9. ROWENA CANO CUANO, 60s + NOEL LEONDRA, nb

JB.8.2.3. MINA CUBINAR GASIS, 20s + AMADO ZANTUA, nb
JB.8.2.3.1. SONIA GASIS ZANTUA, 40s + BENITO ESTRADA, nb
JB.8.2.3.1.1. RUSSELA Z. ESTRADA, 60s + ARTHUR MANLANGIT, nb
JB.8.2.3.1.1.1. MICHAEL ESTRADA MANLANGIT, 80s
JB.8.2.3.1.1.2. FITZGERALD MANLANGIT, 80s
JB.8.2.3.1.2. BOYING ZANTUA ESTRADA, 60s + NOEMI, nb
JB.8.2.3.1.3. RICKY ZANTUA ESTRADA, 60s + RECHILDA, nb
JB.8.2.3.1.4. JOSEPH ZANTUA ESTRADA, 70s + CHRISTY, nb

JB.8.2.3.2. EMELITA GASIS ZANTUA, 40s + RICARDO REMPOLA, nb
JB.8.2.3.2.1. ROLANDO ZANTUA REMPOLA, 60s
JB.8.2.3.2.2. RAMIL ZANTUA REMPOLA, 60s + HENEDINE IBEAS, nb
JB.8.2.3.2.2.1. MENNEN JOYCE COLLIN IBEAS REMPOLA, 80s
JB.8.2.3.2.2.2. JOHN RHENIEL IBEAS REMPOLA, 80s
JB.8.2.3.2.3. EMERITA ZANTUA REMPOLA, 60s + ROLLY LORENZO, nb
JB.8.2.3.2.3.1. ZURENE REMPOLA LORENZO, 80s
JB.8.2.3.2.3.2. ZIZA REMPOLA LORENZO, 80s
JB.8.2.3.2.3.2. ZETRIA REMPOLA LORENZO, 80s
JB.8.2.3.2.4. ARLENE ZANTUA REMPOLA, 60s + CZAR LICAS, nb
JB.8.2.3.2.4.1. TROY CHRISTOPHER REMPOLA LICAS, 80s

(Message: Dina Rempola
Email: dina1990@t-online.de
Date: Wed Feb 21 05:41:17 GMT-12:00 2007
Hi! Nabasa ko ang apelyido ko diyan na Rempola, baka may mga
relatives ako diyan. Iyong pong libro ng kapatid kong si Erwin Rempola
ay available na online sa www.amazon.com the title is "Discovering True
Wealth", suportahan naman natin itong kadugo at kalahi natin. Mabalos
at Mabuhay to all. From Dina Rempola (for editing- but name Dina
Rempola is missing here)

JB.8.2.3.3. PEPITO GASIS ZANTUA, 40s + HERMINIA, nb
JB.8.2.3.3.1. KATRINA HERMINIA ZANTUA, 60s

JB.8.2.3.4. RENATO GASIS ZANTUA, 40s + NENITA FRANCISCO, nb
JB.8.2.3.4.1. MICHAEL FRANCISCO ZANTUA, 60s
JB.8.2.3.4.2. IAN FRANCISCO ZANTUA, 60s
JB.8.2.3.4.3. SHAYNE FRANCISCO ZANTUA, 60s

JB.8.2.3.5. MEDEL GASIS ZANTUA, 50s + EVANGELINE GUREA, nb
JB.8.2.3.5.1. MEDELYN GUREA ZANTUA, 70s + ALLAN VILLALUZ, nb
JB.8.2.3.5.1.1. ALLEN CHRISTOPHER ZANTUA VILLALUZ, 90s
JB.8.2.3.5.2. JEAN GUREA ZANTUA, 70s + ARIES ESTANISLAO, nb
JB.8.2.3.5.2.1. SARAH JOYANTUA ESTANISLAO, 90s
JB.8.2.3.5.3. MAY JANE GUREA ZANTUA, 70s
JB.8.2.3.5.4. RYAN JAY GUREA ZANTUA, 80s
JB.8.2.3.6. NELSON GASIS ZANTUA, 50s + NIEVES LLAGO, nb
JB.8.2.3.6.1. CHRISTINE LLAGO ZANTUA, 70s
JB.8.2.3.6.2. NOEL LLAGO ZANTUA, 70s
JB.8.2.3.6.3. MARICRIS LLAGO ZANTUA, 70s
JB.8.2.3.6.4. NORVIN JOY LLAGO ZANTUA, 80s

JB.8.2.3.7. NESTOR GASIS ZANTUA, 50s + MARILYN PAMESA, nb
JB.8.2.3.7.1. JANSEL PAMESA ZANTUA, 70s
JB.8.2.3.7.2. ANTHONY PAMESA ZANTUA, 70s

JB.8.2.3.8. SUSAN GASIS ZANTUA, 50s + MIKE IGLESIAS, nb
JB.8.2.3.8.1. CLAUDETTE ZANTUA IGLESIAS, 70s

JB.8.2.3.8.2. MIKE LESTER ZANTUA IGLESIAS, 70s
JB.8.2.3.8.3. JASON ZANTUA IGLESIAS, 70s
JB.8.2.3.8.4. SARAH KAYE ZANTUA IGLESIAS, 80s

JB.8.2.3.9. ANNABEL GASIS ZANTUA, 60s + ROLAND MIRANDA, nb
JB.8.2.3.9.1. BILANDO ZANTUA MIRANDA, 80s
JB.8.2.3.9.2. ROWEL ZANTUA MIRANDA, 80s
JB.8.2.3.9.3. GABRIEL ZANTUA MIRANDA, 80s
JB.8.2.3.9.4. EARL ZANTUA MIRANDA, 90s

JB.8.2.3.10. NENITA GAISS ZANTUA, 60s + NELSON MOQUIA, nb
JB.8.2.3.10.1. BERNADETTE ZANTUA MOQUIA, 80s
JB.8.2.3.10.2. NELSON ZANTUA MOQUIA JR, 80s
JB.8.2.3.10.3. BRYAN ZANTUA MOQUIA, 80s

JB.8.2.3.11. MINDA GASIS ZANTUA, 60s + FREDERICK DENNY, nb
JB.8.2.3.11.1. DANIEL ZANTUA DENNY, 80s
JB.8.2.3.12. AMADO GASIS ZANTUA JR, 70s

JB.8.2.4. DOMINGO CUIBINAR GASIS, 20s + RAMONA ZANTUA, nb
JB.8.2.4.1. MERLYN ZANTUA GASIS, 40s + ADOR PURINQUE, nb
JB.8.2.4.1.1. ADOR GASIS PURINQUE JR, 60s
JB.8.2.4.1.2. MARK CHRISTIAN GASIS PURINQUE, 60s
JB.8.2.4.1.3. GRACE LYN GASIS PURINQUE, 60s
JB.8.2.4.1.4. JOJO GASIS PURINQUE, 70s
JB.8.2.4.2. NOEMI ZANTUA GASIS, 40s + NOEL JIMENEZ, nb
JB.8.2.4.2.1. MARLON GASIS JIMENEZ, 60s
JB.8.2.4.2.2.. MARIA LOURDES GASIS JIMENEZ, 60s
JB.8.2.4.2.3. MARIA ROWENA GASIS JIMENEZ, 60s

JB.8.2.4.3. LEONOR ZANTUA GASIS, 40s + RUDY DIONISIO, nb
JB.8.2.4.3.1. LELAND GASIS DIONISIO, 60s
JB.8.2.4.3.2. GERALD GASIS DIONISIO, 60s
JB.8.2.4.3.3. RUDY GASIS DIONISIO JR, 60s
JB.8.2.4.3.4. JOYCE GASIS DIONISIO, 70s
JB.8.2.4.3.5. JAN DARYL GASIS DIONISIO, 70s

JB.8.2.4.4. ARMANDO ZANTUA GASIS, 40s + NOMELITA OBUSAN, nb

JB.8.2.4.4.1. NIEL OBUSAN GASIS, 60s
JB.8.2.4.4.2. JOAN OBUSAN GASIS, 60s
JB.8.2.4.4.3. OLIVER OBUSAN GASIS, 60s

JB.8.2.4.5. DORIS ZANTUA GASIS, 50s + ERIC HOLINGER, nb
JB.8.2.4.5.1. CHRISTOPH GASIS HOLINGER, 70s
JB.8.2.4.5.2. JOHANNES GASIS HOLINGER, 70s

JB.8.2.4.6. ELVIE ZANTUA GASIS, 50s + ENER LAXAMANA, nb
JB.8.2.4.6.1. CHRIS PAOLO GASIS LAXAMANA, 70s
JB.8.2.4.6.2. RABI JAY GASIS LAXAMANA, 70s
JB.8.2.4.6.3. MARCO GASIS LAXAMANA, 70s

JB.8.2.4.7. VIRGINIA ZANTUA GASIS, 50s + HENRY FERNANDEZ, nb
JB.8.2.4.7.1. JADE GASIS FERNANDEZ, 70s
JB.8.2.4.7.2. GINA GASIS FERNANDEZ, 70s
JB.8.2.4.8. JULIE ZANTUA GASIS, 50s + FRANCSICO ALBONIA, nb
JB.8.2.4.8.1. CYRIL JANE GASIS ALBONIA, 70s
JB.8.2.4.8.2. CHERRY ANNE GASIS ALBONIA, 70s
JB.8.2.4.8.3. JOSEPH GASIS ALBONIA, 70s

JB.8.2.4.9. ERLINDA ZANTUA GASIS, 60s

JB.8.2.4.10. DOMINGO ZANTUA GASIS JR, 60s + DOLORES PAJARES, nb
JB.8.2.4.11. RAMON ZANTUA GASIS, 60s + NILDA DELOS SANTOS, nb
JB.8.2.4.11.1. SHERYL KAYE DELOSSANTOS GASIS, 80s
JB.8.2.4.12. HENRY ZANTUA GASIS, 60s + ALONA RECODO RIVERA
JB.8.2.4.12.1. FIONAL EUNICE RIVERA GASIS, 80s

Publisher - Tatay Jobo Elizes

BRANCH NO. 5
BRAULIO JAMITO +
MICHAELA UBINA
(JU - JAMITO-UBINA, 1860s)

Publisher - Tatay Jobo Elizes

JU.1. ISIDORA UBINA JAMITO, 1880s, EARLY RIP

JU.2. VICENTA UBINA JAMITO, 1880s + PLACIDO RAGILES, nb

(Special Note: Placido Ragiles, nb, had a sister, Maria Ragiles, who married Tito Jamito. But this Tito Jamito does not belong to the desendant line of our Patriarch Santiago Jamito. We have no record of Santiago siblings and cousins and cannot trace Tito Jamito line, but being Jamito and taga-Mercedes, he is considered part of the Jamito clan. Their line is JRJ at the end of the book.)

JU.2.0. FE VELASCO RAGILES, 20s (Infant Death - Not counted)

JU.2.1. PIO JAMITO RAGILES, 1900s + ISABEL VELASCO, nb

JU.2.1.1. GIL VELASCO RAGILES, 1924-2004 + ILUMINADA VARGAS, nb,1924
JU.2.1.1.1. ARIEL VARGAS RAGILES, 1949 + BEATRICE-BETH BARBOZA, nb JU.2.1.1.1.1. MABEL BARBOZA RAGILES
JU.2.1.1.1.2. MARIEL BARBOZA RAGILES
JU.2.1.1.1.3. MICHAEL BARBOZA RAGILES
JU.2.1.1.1.4. GALE BARBOZA RAGILES
JU.2.1.1.1.5. MARY JANE BARBOZA RAGILES
JU.2.1.1.1.6. ANGELICA BARBOZA RAGILES
JU.2.1.1.1.7. MARVIN BARBOZA RAGILES

JU.2.1.1.2. BENJAMIN VARGAS RAGILES, 1950 + EDNA GONZALES, nb, 1956
JU.2.1.1.3. CARLOS VARGAS RAGILES, 1953 + WINDY MAE RYES, nb
JU.2.1.1.3.1. CELIA LUZ
JU.2.1.1.3.1.1. CASPER

JU.2.1.1.4. DENNIS VARGAS RAGILES, 1958
JU.2.1.1.5. EDNA VARGAS RAGILES, 1964 + HUSBAND SURNAME, nb
JU.2.1.1.5.1. WYNONA RAGILES-SURNAME

Publisher - Tatay Jobo Elizes

JU.2.1.1.5.2. BREN RAGILES-SURNAME

JU.2.1.2. VICENTA VELASCO RAGILES, 20s + MELANIO ALCONCEL, nb
JU.2.1.2.1. ISABELITA RAGILES ALCONCEL, 40s
JU.2.1.2.2. MELINDA RAGILES ALCONCEL, 40s
JU.2.1.2.3. RAUL RAGILES ALCONCEL, 40s

JU.2.1.3. NORA VELASCO RAGILES, 20s + MAMERTO CASTILLO, nb
JU.2.1.3.1. EARL RAGILES CASTILLO, 40s
JU.2.1.3.2. ANNE RAGILES CASTILLO, 40s
JU.2.1.3.3. DELICIA RAGILES CASTILLO, 40s
JU.2.1.3.4. CHIE RAGILES CASTILLO, 40s
JU.2.1.3.5. LANIE RAGILES CASTILLO, 50s

JU.2.1.4. PLACIDO VELASCO RAGILES, 20s + RAYMUNDA, nb
JU.2.1.4.1. SUSAN RAYMUNDA RAGILES, 40s
JU.2.1.4.2. SYLVIA RAYMUNDA RAGILES, 40s
JU.2.1.4.3. SAMUEL RAYMUNDA RAGILES, 40s

JU.2.1.5. MARIA VELASCO RAGILES, 30s + ARSENIO CABALLERO, nb
JU.2.1.5.1. MARIA HEIDI RAGILES CABALLERO, 50s
JU.2.1.5.2. LOU RAGILES CABALLERO, 50s
JU.2.1.5.3. CRISTINA RAGILES CABALLERO, 50s
JU.2.1.5.4. GRACE RAGILES CABALLERO, 60s
JU.2.1.5.5. RAYMOND RAGILES CABALLERO, 60s

JU.2.1.6. ESTER VELASCO RAGILES, 30s + HUSBAND, nb
JU.2.1.6.1. ROBERTO RAGILES-SURNAME, 50s
JU.2.1.6.2. PIA RAGILES-SURNAME, 50s
JU.2.1.6.3. REY MANUEL RAGILES-SURNAME, 50s

JU.2.2. BERNARDINO JAMITO RAGILES, 1900s, RIP

JU.2.3. CANDIDA JAMITO RAGILES, 1900s + ALEJO BARRIOS, nb

JU.2.3.1. NELLY RAGILES BARRIOS, 20s + JOSE VALENZUELA, nb

Publisher - Tatay Jobo Elizes

JU.2.3.1.1. ADELFA CANDIDA BARRIOS VALENZUELA, 40s + FROILINDO VILLALUZ, nb
(Message June 9/11: Adelfa V. Villaluz, fsimer_villaluz@yahoo.com.ph: Pls add our youngest son, FROILINDO V. VILLALUZ JR. Thank and God bless. Adelfa)

JU.2.3.1.1.1. FSIMER JOHN VALENZUELA VLLALUZ, 60s
JU.2.3.1.1.2. FELICE ANGELOU VALENZUELA VILLALUZ, 60s
JU.2.3.1.1.3. FROILINDO VALENZUELA VILLALUZ JR. 70s
JU.2.3.1.2. MAILA BARRIOS VALENZUELA, 40s

JU.2.3.2. NILDA RAGILES BARRIOS, 20s + EUSEBIO GERIO, nb
JU.2.3.2.1. EMERENCIANA BARRIOS GERIO, 40s *mgbalico@yahoo.com* **+ VICTOR BALICO, nb,** *vabsouth@yahoo.com*
JU.2.3.2.1.1. KARL VINCENT BARRIOS GERIO BALICO, 60s
JU.2.3.2.1.2. KEVIN MATTHEW BARRIOS GERIO BALICO, 60s
JU.2.3.2.1.3. KRISTINNE ANGELA BARRIOS GERIO BALICO, 60s

JU.2.3.2.2. DANNY BARRIOS GERIO, 40s
JU.2.3.2.3. EUSEBIO BARRIOS GERIO JR, 50s + WIFE(nb)
JU.2.3.2.3.1. KEVIN GERIO, 70s
JU.2.3.2.3.2. BRYAN GERIO, 70s

JU.2.3.2.4. NYMPHA BARRIOS GERIO, 50s
JU.2.3.2.5. PERCIVAL BARRIOS GERIO, 50s

JU.2.3.3. TEODORO RAGILES BARRIOS (DOROY), 30s + ELENA SANTOS, nb
JU.2.3.3.1. POCHOLO SANTOS BARRIOS, 50s
JU.2.3.3.2. ALVIN SANTOS BARRIOS, 50s, RIP
JU.2.3.3.3. POMPIDOU SANTOS BARRIOS, 50s + CECILLE, nb
JU.2.3.3.4. MARCIAL SANTOS BARRIOS, 60s
JU.2.3.3.5. MELCHOR SANTOS BARRIOS, 60s

JU.2.3.4. ALEJO RAGILES BARRIOS JR, 30s

JU.2.3.5. FE RAGILES BARRIOS, 30s + ROGARDO CHAVEZ, nb
JU.2.3.5.1. AGNES BARRIOS CHAVEZ, 50s
JU.2.3.5.2. ALEX RAYMOND BARRIOS CHAVEZ, 50s

JU.2.3.5.3. RICARDO BARRIOS CHAVEZ, 50s

JU.2.4. FELINO JAMITO RAGILES, 20s + MARIA CONSUELO, nb

JU.2.4.1. ELY CONSUELO RAGILES, 40s + RAUL GOMEZ, nb
JU.2.4.1.1. GISELA RAGILES GOMEZ, 60s + NESTOR MORENO, nb
JU.2.4.1.1.1. GIMME GOMEZ MORENO, 80s

JU.2.4.1.2. MARIA TERESA RAGILES GOMEZ, 60s
JU.2.4.1.3. GENY RAGILES GOMEZ, 60s + RIC BUAN, nb
JU.2.4.1.4. RAULITO RAGILES GOMEZ, 60s + JOCELYN, nb
JU.2.4.1.4.1. JAKE JOCELYN GOMEZ, 80s
JU.2.4.1.4.2. RIZ-JOY JOCELYN GOMEZ, 80s
JU.2.4.1.4.3. PAOLO JOCELYN GOMEZ, 80s
JU.2.4.1.4.4. DAVE JOCELYN GOMEZ, 90s

JU.2.4.1.5. NELSON RAGILES GOMEZ, 70s + MABEL, nb
JU.2.4.1.5.1. JANINE MABEL GOMEZ, 90s
JU.2.4.1.5.2. PET MABEL GOMEZ, 90s
JU.2.4.1.5.3. ANDREI MABEL GOMEZ, 90s

JU.2.4.1.6. AGNES RAGILES GOMEZ, 70s + EDUARDO ORBILLO, nb
JU.2.4.1.6.1. AUSTIN GOMEZ ORBILLO, 90s
JU.2.4.1.6.2. JUSTIN GOMEZ ORBILLO, 90s
JU.2.4.1.6.3. KEVIN GOMEZ ORBILLO, 90s

JU.2.4.1.7. EDGAR RAGILES GOMEZ, 70s + ANNA MARIE, nb
JU.2.4.1.7.1. HAZEL ANNA-MARIE GOMEZ, 90s
JU.2.4.1.7.2. CHARMAINE ANNA-MARIE GOMEZ, 90s
JU.2.4.1.7.3. ABEGAIL ANNA-MARIE GOMEZ, 90s

JU.2.4.1.8. MELVIN RAGILES GOMEZ, 70s + MIA, nb
JU.2.4.1.8.1. MICO MIA GOMEZ, 90s
JU.2.4.1.8.2. MIKE MIA GOMEZ, 90s
JU.2.4.2. NOEMI CONSUELO RAGILES, 20s + MANUEL RAMORES, nb
JU.2.4.2.1. ERMA RAGILES RAMORES, 1950s + ARMANDO MARQUEZ, 1943, nb

JU.2.4.2.1.1. MICHAEL RAMORES MARQUEZ, 1970s + LAURICE
JOY,1978, nb
JU.2.4.2.1.1.1. RENCIO LOUIS MIGUEL MARQUEZ, 2000
JU.2.4.2.1.1.2. REENA LUCHAEL MARQUEZ, 2001
JU.2.4.2.1.2. ALBERT RAMORES MARQUEZ, 1970S + MARICEL, 1979, nb
JU.2.4.2.1.2.1. MICOLE JAN JOSEPH MARQUEZ, 2002
JU.2.4.2.1.2.1. MIKYLEBON ALBERT MARQUEZ, 2007
JU.2.4.2.1.3. JENNIFER RAMOREZ MARQUEZ, 1980
(*jenifer_ramores_r@yahoo.com -- corrections came from her, dated
09/13/08, all names from Noemi Consuelo Ragiles-Ramores (JU.2.4.2.) up
to Jane Erika Ramores Cosio (JU.2.4.2.6.1.)*)

JU.2.4.2.1.4. RANDOLF RAMORES MARQUEZ, 1984
JU.2.4.2.1.5. JENMAR FRANCESCA RAMORES MARQUEZ, 1997

JU.2.4.2.2. EVELYN RAGILES RAMORES, 1050s + OSCAR RUALES, nb
JU.2.4.2.2.1. FROILAN RAMORES RUALES, 1977 + GEMMA, nb
JU.2.4.2.2.1.1. FROIEKARL LOUISE AIGZHENNE RUALES, 2002
JU.2.4.2.2.1.2. ASHLEY JEWEL RUALES, 2004?
JU.2.4.2.2.2. SUZETT RUALES, 1978 + HERMELO, nb
JU.2.4.2.2.3. JED ALVIN RUALES, 1979?

JU.2.4.2.3. EDUARDO RAGILES RAMORES, 40s + TERESITA, nb
JU.2.4.2.3.1. ROSALIA TERESITA RAMORES, 60s
JU.2.4.2.3.2. RONALD TERESITA RAMORES, 60s
JU.2.4.2.3.3. ROSELE TERESITA RAMORES, 60s
JU.2.4.2.3.4. ROSE ANN TERESITA RAMORES, 70s
JU.2.4.2.3.5. DIMPLE TERESITA RAMORES, 70s

JU.2.4.2.4. RICARDO RAGILES RAMORES, 40s + ANDREA, nb
JU.2.4.2.4.1. JONALYN ANDREA RAMORES, 60s
JU.2.4.2.4.2. JASON ANDREA RAMORES, 60s
JU.2.4.2.4.3. JORDAN ANDREA RAMORES, 60s
JU.2.4.2.4.4. JULIE ANN ANDREA RAMORES, 70s
JU.2.4.2.5. EMMANUEL RAGILES RAMORES, 50s + WIFE
JU.2.4.2.5.1. EMALIZA RAMORES
JU.2.4.2.5.2. JELENE RAMOES
JU.2.4.2.5.3. JEMUEL RAMORES

Publisher - Tatay Jobo Elizes

JU.2.4.2.5.4. JERICA RAMORES

JU.2.4.2.6. ELEANOR RAGILES RAMORES, 50s + JOJO COSIO, nb
JU.2.4.2.6.1. JANE ERIKA (JAKA) RAMORES COSIO, 70s
    --- above list as corrected by Jennifer Ramores, JU.2.4.2.1.3. ----

JU.2.4.3. ELVIGIA CONSUELO RAGILES, 20s + BALDOMERO RANADA, nb
JU.2.4.3.1. CECILIA RAGILES RANADA, 40s, RIP

JU.2.4.3.2. REGINA RAGILES RANADA, 40s + VICENTE ARAGON, nb
JU.2.4.3.2.1. DARWIN RANADA ARAGON, 60s
JU.2.4.3.2.2. RHEA RANADA ARAGON, 60s
JU.2.4.3.2.3. JOSEPH RANADA ARAGON, 60s
JU.2.4.3.2.4. VINCENT RANADA ARAGON, 70s

JU.2.4.3.3. AMELIA RAGILES RANADA, 40s + SIMEON ACITUNA, nb
JU.2.4.3.3.1. SUZIE RANADA ACITUNA, 60s
JU.2.4.3.3.2. ANGELICA RANADA ACITUNA, 60s
JU.2.4.3.3.3. SILVESTER RANADA ACITUNA, 60s
JU.2.4.3.3.4. ARA RANADA ACITUNA, 70s
JU.2.4.3.3.5. ZANDREX RANADA ACITUNA, 70s

JU.2.4.3.4. ROLANDO RAGILES RANADA, 40s + TERESITA, nb
JU.2.4.3.4.1. ANGELO TERESITA RANADA, 60s
JU.2.4.3.4.2. RUEL TERESITA RANADA, 60s
JU.2.4.3.4.3. MARY ANN TERESITA RANADA, 60s
JU.2.4.3.4.4. JUN-JUN TERESITA RANADA, 70s
JU.2.4.3.4.5. MARY JANE TERESITA RANADA, 70s
JU.2.4.3.4.6. MARY GRACE TERESITA RANADA, 70s

JU.2.4.3.5. LENY RAGILES RANADA, 50s + EPIFANIA TAPALES, nb
JU.2.4.3.5.1. ZENDRIZ TAPALES RANADA, 70s
JU.2.4.3.5.2. ZANDREX TAPALES RANADA, 70s

JU.2.4.3.6. MARTHY RAGILES RANADA, 50s + ARNEL QUIA, nb
JU.2.4.3.6.1. MICO RANADA QUIA, 70s
JU.2.4.3.6.2. PATRICK RANADA QUIA, 70s

JU.2.4.3.6.3. NIEVES RANADA QUIA, 70s
JU.2.4.3.6.4. JONATHAN RANADA QUIA, 80s
JU.2.4.3.6.5. BEA RANADA QUIA, 80s

JU.2.4.3.7. BALDOMERO RAGILES RANADA JR, 50s + CANDELARIA, nb
JU.2.4.3.7.1. GHEA CANDELARIA RANADA, 70s

JU.2.4.3.8. CATHERINE RAGILES RANADA, 50s + JEFF MACALINO, nb
JU.2.4.3.8.1. KOLIN RANADA MACALINO, 70s

JU.2.4.4. REMEDIOS CONSUELO RAGILES, 20s + ANANIAS YANILLA, nb
JU.2.4.4.1. MAYONELO RAGILES YANILLA, 40s
JU.2.4.4.2. WIVINA RAGILES YANILLA, 40s + HUSBAND (*Wivina is very close friend of Emily Jamito Espanol-Derry of the JRJ-Jamito-Ragiles-Jamito Tree at the end of the book*)
JU.2.4.4.2.1. AJ YANILLA-SURNAME, 60s

JU.2.4.4.3. GLECIE RAGILES YANILLA, 40s
JU.2.4.4.4. AILEEN RAGILES YANILLA, 50s

JU.2.4.5. ORFELINA CONSUELO RAGILES,40s + WILFREDO PALADO, nb
JU.2.4.5.1. RONELO RAGILES PALADO, 60s + ERLINDA SENIS, nb
JU.2.4.5.1.1. MARIE JO SENIS PALADO, 90s
JU.2.4.5.1.2. JOMARI SENIS PALADO, 90s
JU.2.4.5.1.3. MARICRIS SENIS PALADO, 02s

JU.2.4.5.2. ROSELA RAGILES PALADO, 60s + RONILO RAFER, nb
JU.2.4.5.3. ROWELA RAGILES PALADO, 70s + IRVING EBOJO, nb
(*Palado branch corrected by Rowela 3/16/09), nheng10@yahoo.com*
JU.2.4.5.3.1. IRRA ANGELA PALADO EBOJO, 08s

JU.2.4.6. CELENIA CONSUELO RAGILES, + BERNARDO GONZALES, nb
JU.2.4.6.1. GONGON RAGILES GONZALES, 50s
JU.2.4.6.2. JASPER RAGILES GONZALES, 50s

JU.2.5. LEONORA JAMITO RAGILES, 10s + PRIMO MAGANA, nb

Publisher - Tatay Jobo Elizes

JU.2.5.1. LEOVINA RAGILES MAGANA, 30s
JU.2.5.2. PRIMARION RAGILES MAGANA, 30s + TOMEO PUSO, nb
JU.2.5.3. NARDING RAGILES MAGANA, 30s
JU.2.5.4. LINA RAGILES MAGANA, 30s
JU.2.5.5. DIVINA RAGILES MAGANA, 40s
JU.2.5.6. LUCER RAGILES MAGANA, 40s
JU.2.5.7. AIDA RAGILES MAGANA, 40s
JU.2.5.8. ANDY RAGILES MAGANA, 50s
JU.1.5.9. DINO RAGILES MAGANA, 50s

JU.2.6. PAZ JAMITO RAGILES, 10s + ANDRES MARQUEZ, nb. (*NANA PANG MARQUEZ. IS ANOTHER AUTHOR OF PREFACE-PAGHAHANDOG - NOBENARYA.*)

JU.2.6.1. ROSARIO RAGILES MARQUEZ, 30s + TOTO TORRES, nb
JU.2.6.1.1. BURT MARQUEZ TORRES, 50s
JU.2.6.1.2. PAZ MARQUEZ TORRES, 50s
JU.2.6.1.3. SYLVIA MARQUEZ TORRES, 50s + JUANCHO LAS, nb
JU.2.6.1.3.1. JUAN CARLO TORRES LAS, 70s

JU.2.6.1.4. BALAGTAS MARQUEZ TORRES, 60s

JU.2.6.2. RAMON RAGILES MARQUEZ, 30s + MERLY, nb
JU.2.6.2.1. CHRISELDA MERLY MARQUEZ, 50s
JU.2.6.2.2. RICO MERLY MARQUEZ, 50s
JU.2.6.2.3. ANDREW MERLY MARQUEZ, 50s
JU.2.6.2.4. HARRY MERLY MARQUEZ, 60s

JU.2.6.3. YOLLY RAGILES MARQUEZ, 30s
JU.2.6.4. ERLINDA RAGILES MARQUEZ, 30s + MONICO IMPERIAL, nb (RAUL?)
JU.2.6.4.1. RAYMOND MARQUEZ IMPERIAL, 50s
JU.2.6.4.2. JASMIN MARQUEZ IMPERIAL, 50s + JOSEPH AGRAVENT, nb
JU.2.6.4.2.1. HURT THOMAS IMPERIAL AGRAVENT, 70s
JU.2.6.4.3. UNKNOWN MARQUEZ IMPERIAL, 50s
JU.2.6.4.4. DOMINQUE MARQUEZ IMPERIAL, 60s
JU.2.6.5. BELLA RAGILES MARQUEZ, 40s + HUSBAND(nb)
JU.2.6.5.1. ROMINA MARQUEZ-SURNAME, 60s

JU.2.6.5.2. MARK MARQUEZ-SURNAME, 60s
JU.2.6.5.3. RAMONA MARQUEZ-SURNAME, 60s

JU.3. POMPOSA UBINA JAMITO, 1880s + VICENTE LEGASPI, nb

JU.3.1. ELENA JAMITO LEGASPI, 1900s, RIP

JU.3.2. MARIA JAMITO LEGASPI, 1900s + ESPERIDION CONTRERAS, nb *(EX-TALISAY MAYOR)*

JU.3.2.1. GODOFREDO LEGASPI CONTRERAS, 20s+ CONSTANCIA RAVAGO, nb
(Godofredo was hero, killed together with Bintao during Japanese time)
JU.3.2.1.1, GODOFREDO RAVAGO CONTRERAS JR, 40s + WIFE JURIS, nb
JU.3.2.1.1.1. GLENN JURIS CONTRERAS, 60s
JU.3.2.1.1.2. NORLITO JURIS CONTRERAS, 60s, RIP
JU.3.2.1.1.3. EDUARDO JURIS CONTRERAS, 60s

JU.3.2.2. NATIVIDAD LEGASPI CONTRERAS, 20s + FELIX BACUNO(nb)
JU.3.2.2.1. MARIA CONTRERAS BACUNO, 40s + ERNESTO PENA(nb)
JU.3.2.2.1.1. DONDON BACUNO PENA, 60s
JU.3.2.2.1.2. MAITA BACUNO PENA, 60s
JU.3.2.2.1.3. MAILA BACUNO PENA, 60s

JU.3.2.2.2. LUISA CONTRERAS BACUNO, 40s + ORLANDO PADILLA, nb
JU.3.2.2.3. ALICIA CONTRERAS BACUNO, 40s + OVIDIO EBUENGA, nb

JU.3.2.2.3.1. OVIDIO BACUNO EBUENGA II, 60s
(Message: Date: Wed Nov 5 22:46:07 GMT-12:00 2008
Nice web site, my name is there, under the JU code cool but my real
name is Ovidio B. Ebuenga II not Jun)

JU.3.2.2.3.2. REX BACUNO EBUENGA, 60s

JU.3.2.3. ILUMINADA LEGASPI CONTRERAS, 20s + FEDERICO

PEMPENA, nb
JU.3.2.3.1. MANOLITO CONTRERAS PEMPENA, 40s
JU.3.2.3.2. LUZVIMINDA CONTRERAS PEMPENA, 40s
JU.3.2.3.3. GODOFREDO CONTRERAS PEMPENA, 40s
JU.3.2.3.4. ARACELI CONTRERAS PEMPENA, 50s

JU.3.2.4. GUMERSINDO LEPASPI CONTRERAS, 30s + GLORIA VILLAROSA, nb
JU.3.2.4.1. GENIA VILLAROSA CONTRERAS, 50s

JU.3.2.5. LILIA LEPASPI CONTRERAS, 30s

JU.3.3. RAMON JAMITO LEGASPI, 1900s + CONCEPCION JACOBO, nb *(Ramon was Talisay Mayor before and during Japanese time)*

JU.3.3.1. CONRADO JACOBO LEGASPI, 20s + CECILIA LARGO, nb
JU.3.3.1.1. ENGELBERTO LARGO LEGASPI, 40s
JU.3.3.1.2. SHIELA LARGO LEGASPI, 40s
JU.3.3.1.3. CONRADO LARGO LEGASPI JR, 40s

JU.4. TOMASA UBINA JAMITO, 1890s + PLACIDO ABRIOL, nb

JU.4.1. BEATRIZ JAMITO ABRIOL, 10s + DOMINADOR PADILLA, nb *(Beatriz was one of the signatories to the Nobenaryo Del Rosario)*

JU.4.1.1. CONRADO ABRIOL PADILLA, 30s + PRECY DEL ROSARIO, nb
JU.4.1.1.1. CAROLYN DELROSARIO PADILLA, 50s
JU.4.1.1.2. MARIE DELROSARIO PADILLA, 50s
JU.4.1.1.3. ANA MARIE DELROSARIO PADILLA, 50s
JU.4.1.1.4. MICHELLE DELROSARIO PADILLA, 60s
JU.4.1.1.5. BEATRIZ DELROSARIO PADILLA, 60s

JU.4.1.2. AMPARO ABRIOL PADILLA, 30s + JEROME BENOZA, nb
JU.4.1.2.1. JEREMY BENOZA BENOZA, 50s

Publisher - Tatay Jobo Elizes

JU.4.1.3. FILIPINA ABRIOL PADILLA, 30s + OSCAR GUINTO, nb
JU.4.1.4. RUBEN ABRIOL PADILLA, 30s + PACITA CORPUS, nb
JU.4.1.4.1. KRISTOPHER C. PADILLA, b.1992

JU.4.1.5. MARIA THERESA ABRIOL PADILLA, 40s

JU.5. EUSTACIA UBINA JAMITO, 1890s + TOMAS MANCENIDO, nb

JU.5.1. CORNELIO JAMITO MANCENIDO, 10s + APOLONIA VELASCO, nb

JU.5.1.1. TOMAS VELASCO MANCENIDO, 30s + LILIA ABRIOL, nb
(Tom was Talisay Mayor in the 1980s)

JU.5.1.1.1. FERDINAND ABRIOL MANCENIDO, 50s + ELAINE VELASCO, nb
Malmon77@yahoo.com
JU.5.1.1.1.1. MEGAN VELASCO MANCENIDO, 70s
JU.5.1.1.1.2. AMANDA VELASCO MANCENIDO, 70s

JU.5.1.1.2. TOMAS ABRIOL MANCENIDO III, 50s
JU.5.1.1.3. NORMAN ABRIOL MANCENIDO, 60s
JU.5.1.1.4. LAINE ABRIOL MANCENIDO, 60s + DON ROSALES, nb
JU.5.1.1.5. DONOVAN ABRIOL MANCENIDO, 60s
JU.5.1.1.6. ERIC ABRIOL MANCENIDO, 70s
JU.5.1.1.7. RICA ABRIOL MANCENIDO, 80s
JU.5.1.2. MABEL VELASCO MANCENIDO, 30s + BUTCH REBODOS, nb
JU.5.1.2.1.BUTCHIE MANCENIDO REBODOS, 50s + WIFE, nb
JU.5.1.2.1. LEE REBODOS, 50s + KIEU, nb
JU.5.1.2.2.1. KEVIN KIEU REBODOS, 70s .
JU.5.1.2.2.2. CONNER KIEU REBODOS, 70s

JU.5.1.2.3. KIMBERLY REBODOS, 60s + TODD SLINKARD, nb
JU.5.1.2.4. MACKENZIE REBODOS, 60s

JU.5.1.3. AMABLE-TOTOY VELASCO MANCENIDO, 30s + VIRGIE, nb

Publisher - Tatay Jobo Elizes

JU.5.1.3.1. AMABLE VIRGIE MANCENIDO JR, 50s + WINNIE, nb
JU.5.1.3.2. JENNIFER VIRGIE MANCENIDO, 50s
JU.5.1.3.3. JONATHAN VIRGIE MANCENIDO, 50s

JU.5.1.4. CORNELIO VELASCO MANCENIDO JR, 40s + CORAZON ANTONIO, nb
JU.5.1.4.1. PATRICK ANTONIO MANCENIDO, 60s
JU.5.1.4.2. CHRISTOPHER ANTONIO MANCENIDO, 60s

JU.5.2. LICERIO JAMITO MANCENIDO, 10s(Atty/Judge)RIP + MELANIA GARDE, nb

JU.5.2.1. MELINDA GARDE MANCENIDO,40s + ALFREDO NICOLAS, nb
JU.5.2.1.1. ALLAN MANCENIDO NICOLAS, 60s + LURA DIETRICH, nb
JU.5.2.1.1.1. ZERMETT DIETRICH NICOLAS (RIP), 80s
JU.5.2.1.1.2. ANIKA DIETRICH NICOLAS, 80s
JU.5.2.1.1.3. AUSTIN DIETRICH NICOLAS, 90s

JU.5.2.1.2. ALMA ROCHELLE MANCENIDO NICOLAS, 60s + DAVID GASKELL, nb
JU.5.2.1.2.1. ANDREW NICOLAS GASKELL, 80s

JU.5.2.1.3. ARNOLD MANCENIDO NICOLAS,70s
JU.5.2.1.4. ANNAZARINA MANCENIDO NICOLAS, 70s
JU.5.2.1.5. ALFRED MANCENIDO NICOLAS, 80s
JU.5.2.2. SUSAN GARDE MANCENIDO, 40s + ALEXANDER RODRIGUEZ, nb
JU.5.2.2.1. ANNA LIZA MANCENIDO RODRIGUEZ, 60s + RUSSELL YOUNG, nb
JU.5.2.2.1.1. TAYLOR ANGELIQUE RODRIGUEZ YOUNG, 80s

JU.5.2.2.2. ANDREI ROMMEL MANCENIDO RODRIGUEZ, 60s + ARLENE GRACE PULIDO, nb *(Both MD's)*
JU.5.2.2.3. DEOGRACIAS ANTON MANCENIDO RODRIGUEZ, 70s

JU.5.2.3. DANILO GARDE MANCENIDO, 50s + AIDA, nb
JU.5.2.3.1. MICHAEL AIDA MANCENIDO, 70s
JU.5.2.3.2. DION AIDA MANCENIDO, 70s

Publisher - Tatay Jobo Elizes

JU.5.2.3.3. AIDYN AIDA MANCENIDO, 80s + MICHAEL MILLS, nb

JU.5.2.4. LICERIO GARDE MANCENIDO JR, 50s + LINDA, nb
JU.5.2.4.1. JONATHAN LINDA MANCENIDO, 80s
JU.5.2.4.2. JENJEN LINDA MANCENIDO,80s + MARK ALTOVIROS, nb
JU.5.2.4.2.1. PORTIA MANCENIDO ALTOVIROS, 90s
JU.5.2.4.3. JHAJHA LINDA MANCENIDO, 80s
JU.5.2.4.4. JOAN LINDA MANCENIDO, 80s
JU.5.2.4.5. JOHANEZ LINDA MANCENIDO, 80s

JU.5.3. LIGAYA JAMITO MANCENIDO-NANA LILING, 1919-2010 +
AUGUSTO DELOS ANGELES, nb, RIP

JU.5.3.1. MATIAS(MATCHIE) M. DELOSANGELES, 40s(RIP) + EDITH
DELACRUZ, nb
JU.5.3.1.1. EMILAINE DELACRUZ DELOSANGELES, 70s + BRAD
CONLEY, nb
JU.5.3.1.1.1. ZACHARY DELOSANGELES CONLEY, 90s
JU.5.3.1.1.2. JACOB DELOSANGELES CONLEY, 90s

JU.5.3.1.2. EMERISSA DELACRUZ DELOSANGELES, 70s +ANDREW
BABIN, nb
JU.5.3.1.2.1. TYLER DELOSANGELES BABIN,90s
JU.5.3.1.2.2. RYAN DELOSANGELES BABIN,90s
JU.5.3.1.3. EMERALD DELACRUZ DELOSANGELES, 70s + COLIN LACEY,
nb
JU.5.3.1.3.1. ISABEL DELOSANGELES LACEY, 90s

JU.5.3.1.4. MARIGAY DELACRUZ DELOSANGELES,80s + STEFAN
BOCKHOP, nb
JU.5.3.1.4.1. HANNAH DELOSANGELES BOCKHOP, 00s
JU.5.3.2. ANTONIO MANCENIDO DELOSANGELES, 40s + LORNA SALES,
nb
JU.5.3.3. AUGUSTO(TITO) MANCENIDO DELOSANGELES,40s +
ROSARIO URSOLINO, nb
JU.5.3.3.1. ANGELO URSOLINO DELOSANGELES, 70s
JU.5.3.3.2. ALLAN URSOLINO DELOSANGELES,80s
JU.5.3.3.3. ARNOLD URSOLINO DELOSANGELES, 80s

JU.5.3.4. RAUL MANCENIDO DELOS ANGELES, 50s + SONIA SALAZAR, nb
JU.5.3.4.1. WENDELL SALAZAR DELOSANGELES, 80s + RHODALYN, nb
JU.5.3.4.1.1. ANDREA RHODALYN DELOSANGELES, 00s
JU.5.3.4.1.2. JOHNJOHN RHODALYN DELOSANGELS, 00s
JU.5.3.4.2. CLAUDETTE SALAZAR DELOSANGELES, 80s + HERBERT CAPISTRANO, nb
JU.5.3.4.3. CEDRIC SALAZAR DELOSANGELES, 80s

JU.5.3.5. MERCEDES MANCENIDO DELOSANGELES, 50s + BENJAMIN JOAQUIN, nb
JU.5.3.5.1. FROILAN DELOSANGELES JOAQUIN, 80s
JU.5.3.5.2. LEA DELOSANGELES JOAQUIN, 80s + REID LIND, nb

JU.6. ANTONINO UBINA JAMITO, 1890s + FRANCISCA VARGAS, nb

JU.6.1. DR.MAGNO VARGAS JAMITO, 10s(RIP) + HELEN ELLA, nb

JU.6.1.1. DR.MAGNO ELLA JAMITO JR (RIP), 30s + JULIE,nb, W1 + W2
JU.6.1.1.1. BOY JAMITO III (JULIE'S)
JU.6.1.1.2. CHILD1 JAMITO (W2)
JU.6.1.1.3. CHILD2 JAMITO (W2)

JU.6.2. JOSE VARGAS JAMITO, 10s(JUDGE) + EMILIA RAYOS, nb
(Note: Rayos Siblings are (1)Soledad Rayos-Sangcap (2) Juanita Rayos (3) Jose Rayos (4) Bawit Rayos)

JU.6.2.1. EMILY RAYOS JAMITO, 30s + ALEX FERMO, nb
JU.6.2.1.1. ARLENE JAMITO FERMO, 70s + HUSBAND, nb
JU.6.2.1.2. JOHN JOHN JAMITO FERMO, 70s
JU.6.2.1.3. JOJO JAMITO FERMO, 70s + FLOTABEL, nb

JU.6.2.2. JOSIE RAYOS JAMITO, 40s

JU.6.3. CESAR VARGAS JAMITO, 20s + SALVACION EVA, nb

JU.6.3.1. MARYLOU EVA JAMITO,'41 + MR.QUINTO, nb, RIP
JU.6.3.1.1. CHILD 1 JAMITO QUINTO
JU.6.3.1.2. CHILD 2 JAMITO QUINTO
JU.6.3.1.3. CHILD 3 JAMITO QUINTO

JU.6.3.2. ANA EVA JAMITO, 40s + REYNALDO VILLAPOMA, nb
JU.6.3.2.1. REYNALDO JAMITO VILLAPOMA, 60s
JU.6.3.2.2. REYNA JAMITO VILLAPOMA, 60s

JU.6.3.3. BRAULIO-BALPY EVA JAMITO, 40s + EDEN GUARDIAN, nb
JU.6.3.3.1. ANTONINO GUARDIAN JAMITO, 60s
JU.6.3.3.2. JULIUS CESAR GUARDIAN JAMITO, 60s
JU.6.3.3.3. CARLOS GUARDIAN JAMITO, 60s

JU.6.3.4. MARIA EVA VICTORIA JAMITO, 40s
JU.6.3.5. RICARDO EVA JAMITO, 50s
JU.6.3.6. FRANCISCO EVA JAMITO, 50s
JU.6.3.7. MARIA CARMEN (MARICAR) EVA JAMITO,50s + BRUCE GEORGE GATTI, nb
JU.6.3.6.1. CRISTINA MARIE GATTI, b.1985

JU.6.3.7. JOSE-POPOY-JOEY EVA JAMITO, 60s + AMY GALERO, nb
JU.6.3.7.1. MARILEN-MAY GALERO JAMITO, 80s
JU.6.3.7.2. JOSEPH MYLES GALERO JAMITO, 80s
JU.6.3.7.3. JOSEPH MARK GALERO JAMITO, 80s

JU.6.3.8. LORENZO EVA JAMITO, 60s
JU.6.3.9. CESAR TIMEOTEO EVA JAMITO JR, 60s
JU.6.3.10. EMMANUEL EVA JAMITO, 60s

JU.6.4. MARIA VARGAS JAMITO, 20s + JESUS IMPERIAL, nb

JU.6.4.1. RAUL (BOY) JAMITO IMPERIAL, B1946-D2006/9/13 + WIFE, nb
JU.6.4.2. CALO JAMITO IMPERIAL, B1948? + WIFE, nb
JU.6.4.3. ARACELI (BABA) JAMITO IMPERIAL, B1950 + MARIANITO

MEDINA, nb
JU.6.4.3.1. LALA IMPERIAL MEDINA, 70s
JU.6.4.3.2. JAY IMPERIAL MEDINA, 70s
JU.6.4.3.3. BING IMPERIAL MEDINA, 70s
JU.6.4.3.4. BRISH IMPERIAL MEDINA, 70s
JU.6.4.4. DAISY JAMITO IMPERIAL, B1952 + RAMON ROCO, nb,
(bcrother of late Sen.Raul Roco)
JU.6.4.5. EDEN JAMITO IMPERIAL, B1954 + HUSBAND, nb

JU.7. CENONA UBINA JAMITO, 1890s + PETRONILO BITONIO, nb

JU.7.1. CORAZON JAMITO BITONIO, 10s + JOSE BRINAS, nb

JU.7.1.1. ESTRELLA BITONIO BRINAS, 30s + CESAR GUTIERREZ, nb
JU.7.1.2. ROWEL BITONIO BRINAS, 30s + NENA, nb
JU.7.1.3. CARLOS BITONIO BRINAS, 30s, RIP
JU.7.1.4. ANGUSTIA BITONIO BRINAS, 40s + MANUEL, nb

JU.7.2. JESUS JAMITO BITONIO,10s +EPIFANIA PABICO, nb

JU.7.2.1. WILFREDO PABICO BITONIO, 30s
JU.7.2.2. FE PABICO BITONIO, 30s + SERGIO ABONAL, nb
JU.7.2.2.1. JEROME BITONIO ABONAL, 50s + CARMEN F. BERNAD, nb
Jer_abo@yahoo.com.ph
JU.7.2.2.1.1. KASSANDRA PAULA BERNAD ABONAL, '96

JU.7.2.2.2. EDA BITONIO ABONAL, 50s + RUSTICO OCAMPO, nb
JU.7.2.2.2.1. RICARDO ABONAL OCAMPO, 70s
JU.7.2.2.2.2. ROSELDA ABONAL OCAMPO, 70s
JU.7.2.2.2.3. RECHILDA ABONAL OCAMPO, 70s

JU.7.2.2.3. SHIRLEY-BEBOT BITONIO ABONAL, 50s + DOMINADOR ANGELES, nb
JU.7.2.2.3.1. SHIELA ABONAL ANGELES, 70s
JU.7.2.2.3.2. MAYLIN ABONAL ANGELES, 70s

JU.7.2.2.4. SERGIO BITONIO ABONAL JR, 60s + JEAN, nb
JU.7.2.2.4.1. RIO JEAN ABONAL, 80s
JU.7.2.2.4.2. JEANETTE JEAN ABONAL, 80s

JU.7.2.2.5. CHARITY BITONIO ABONAL, 60s + RICKY MANLESES, nb
JU.7.2.2.5.1. KIT ABONAL MANLESES, 80s

JU.7.2.2.6. SERGIO BITONIO ABONAL III, 60s + HELEN MADRONIO, nb
JU.7.2.2.6.1. ERROL MADRIONIO ABONAL, 80s
JU.7.2.2.6.2. ALICE MADRONIO ABONAL, 80s

JU.7.2.2.7. BABY FE BITONIO ABONAL, 70s + ARNEL CARAMOAN, nb
JU.7.2.2.7.1. JESSICA ABONAL CARAMOAN, 90s
JU.7.2.2.7.2. OTOY ABONAL CARAMOAN, 90s
JU.7.2.2.7.3. CHRISTIAN ABONAL CARAMOAN, 90s
JU.7.2.2.7.4. ANGELICA ABONAL CARAMOAN, 00s
JU.7.2.2.7.5. MORENA ABONAL CARAMOAN, 00s
JU.7.2.2.8. JESUS BITONIO ABONAL, 70s + RACHEL, nb
JU.7.2.2.8.1. RACHEL JOY RACHEL ABONAL, 90s

JU.7.3. RUBEN JAMITO BITONIO, 10s + CONCEPCION RAYMUNDO, nb

JU.7.3.1. ERLINDA RAYMUNDO BITONIO, 30s + CELEDONIO BELLEN, nb
JU.7.3.1.1. RICHARD BITONIO BELLEN, 50s + RIZZY, nb
JU.7.3.1.1.1. CHARLEMAIN RIZZY BELLEN, 70s

JU.7.3.1.2. ROWENA BITONIO BELLEN, 50s + ROY SABULARSE, nb
JU.7.3.1.1.2. ROY CHRISTIAN BELLEN SABULARSE, 70s

JU.7.3.1.3. ROMULO BITONIO BELLEN, 50s + MICHELLE MANALO, nb
JU.7.3.1.4. DONOVAN BITONIO BELLEN, 60s

JU.7.3.2. MERLE RAYMUNDO BITONIO, 30s
JU.7.3.3. RODEL RAYMUNDO BITONIO, 30s + ALICIA CHUA, nb
JU.7.3.3.1. HERSEY CHUA BITONIO, 50s
JU.7.3.3.2. MICHELLE CHUA BITONIO, 50s

JU.7.3.4. ALLAN RAYMUNDO BITONIO, 40s + MELINDA ESPANA, nb

Publisher - Tatay Jobo Elizes

JU.7.3.4.1. ALBERTO ESPANA BITONIO, 60s
JU.7.3.4.2. ALVIN ESPANA BITONIO, 60s
JU.7.3.4.3. ALEX ESPANA BITONIO, 60s
JU.7.3.4.4. CLAIRE ESPANA ANTONETTE, 70s
JU.7.3.4.5. ALLAN ESPANA BITONIO JR, 70s

JU.7.3.5. RUBEN RAUMUNDO BITONIO JR, 40s + JOSEFINA AVILA, nb
JU.7.3.5.1. JOVEN AVILA BITONIO, 60s

JU.7.3.6. LEONOR RAYMUNDO BITONIO, 40s, RIP + RICHARD DATOR, nb
JU.7.3.6.1. OFELIA BITONIO DATOR, 60s
JU.7.3.6.2. KATRINA BITONIO DATOR, 60s

JU.7.3.7. IMELDA RAYMUNDO BITONIO, 50s + REYNALD CRUZ, nb
JU.7.3.7.1. JOHN MARIZE BITONIO CRUZ, 70s
JU.7.3.7.2. FRANCIA BITONIO CRUZ, 70s

JU.7.3.8. ALMA RAYMUNDO BITONIO, 50s + HERMOGENES RODAJE, nb
JU.7.3.8.1. MAC GYVER BITONIO RUDAJE, 70s, *mac_rodaje@yahoo.com*
(Name: mac gyver bitonio rodaje : Email: mac_rodaje@yahoo.com
Date: Sat Mar 4 21:18:20 GMT-12:00 2006
Salamat sa gumawa nitong website. Dahil dito nalaman ko ang mga iba
ko pang mga kapamilya. WOW grabe ang laki pala ng pamilya natin.
Grabe ang mga lolo at lola natin magpadami...heheheheheheh.)

JU.7.3.8.2. JOAN BITONIO RODAJE, 70s
JU.7.3.8.3. JESSICA BITONIO RODAJE, 70s
JU.7.3.8.4. MARY ANNE BITONIO RODAJE, 80s
JU.7.3.8.5. JENNIFER BITONIO RODAJE, 80s
JU.7.3.8.6. HERMOGENES BITONIO RODAJE JR, 80s
JU.7.3.8.7. LOUIE BITONIO RODAJE, 90s

JU.7.4. JOSE JAMITO BITONIO, 20s + FIDELA CUANO, nb

JU.7.4.1. EVELYN CUANO BITONIO, 40s + EDWIN FLORES(nb)
JU.7.4.1.1. CHRISTOPHER BITONIO FLORES, 60s
JU.7.4.1.2. MARIGRACE BITONIO FLORES, 60s

JU.7.4.1.3. DON ERIC BITONIO FLORES, 60s
JU.7.4.1.4. KATRINA BITONIO FLORES, 70s

JU.7.4.2. RENE CUANO BITONIO, 40s + GIGI JIMENEZ, nb
JU.7.4.2.1. DEXTER JIMENEZ BITONIO, 60s
JU.7.4.2.2. DEXTER ALEXANDER JIMENEZ BITONIO, 60s
JU.7.4.2.3. ANALYN JIMENEZ BITONIO, 60s

JU.7.4.3. RADEN CUANO BITONIO, 40s
JU.7.4.4. DARYL CUANO BITONIO, 50s + LOTIE VILLAGARCIA, nb
JU.7.4.5. JUDEL CUANO BITONIO, 50s

BRANCH NO. 6
ANA JAMITO +
RUFINO RAMORES
(JR - JAMITO RAMORES, 1860s)

Publisher - Tatay Jobo Elizes

JR.1. SIMPLICIO RAMORES, 1880s + GERTRUDES MAGANA, nb (W1) + MELIOTONA BARCE, nb (W2)

JR.1.1. NEMESIA MAGANA RAMORES, 1900s + VITO EFONDO, nb

(Message from Ramon V. Efondo : Email: rvefondo@yahoo.com
Date: Sun Dec 28 20:31:32 GMT-12:00 2008
Hi! I'm the son of Engr. Jesus Moreno-Efondo and Grandson of Felicisimo Carranceja-Efondo, who is the son of Miguel Efondo whose father was Fruto Efondo. I entered this amazing site in the hopes of getting connected with the relatives of my great ancestors. I discovered that one Vito Efondo married Nemesia Magana Ramores (Branch 6) and had 7 children. I wish to get connected with their children and be able to get needed information on how Vito Efondo was related to anyone of my relatives above-named.)

JR.1.1.1. MENA RAMORES EFONDO, 20s + LORENZO JALINA, nb

JR.1.1.1.1. JUANITO EFONDO JALINA, 40s + EMILIA DE MATA, nb
JR.1.1.1.2. DOLORES EFONDO JALINA, 40s + JOAQUIN VILLAROSA, nb
JR.1.1.1.3. DOMINGO EFONDO JALINA, 40s + TEODORA PEDIR, nb
JR.1.1.1.4. RICARDO EFONDO JALINA, 40s + EMMA BARIZO, nb
JR.1.1.1.5. ANGEL EFONDO JALINA, 50s + MARILYN ALOC, nb
JR.1.1.1.6. LILIA EFONDO JALINA, 50s + ERNESTO TABOR, nb
JR.1.1.1.7. MELINDA EFONDO JALINA, 50s + CARLITO MAGO nb
JR.1.1.1.8. EMMA EFONDO ALINA, 50s + HENRY RAMPAS, nb
JR.1.1.1.9. ELSA EFONDO JALINA, 60s + RENE LALLO, nb
JR.1.1.1.10. BELEN EFONDO JALINA, 60s + ADONIS BORAC, nb
JR.1.1.1.11. AURORA JALINA, 60s + EMILIA SALVA, nb

JR.1.1.2. NOEMI RAMORES EFONDO, 20s + ELEUTERIO ALBONIA, nb
JR.1.1.2.1. ANICETO EFONDO ALBONIA, 40s, RIP
JR.1.1.2.2. FERNANDO EFONDO ALBONIA, 40s, RIP
JR.1.1.2.3. JESUS EFONDO ALBONIA, 40s, RIP
JR.1.1.2.4. MARIO EFONDO ALBONIA, 40s

JR.1.1.2.5. ANITA EFONDO ALBONIA, 50s
JR.1.1.2.6. REYNALDO EFONDO ALBONIA, 50s
JR.1.1.2.7. NESTOR EFONDO ALBONIA, 50s
JR.1.1.2.8. MELINDA EFONDO ALBONIA, 50s
JR.1.1.2.9. GLORIA EFONDO ALBONIA, 60s

JR.1.1.3. LUZ RAMORES EFONDO, 20s + DOMINGO FREYRA, nb

JR.1.1.4. JAIME RAMORES EFONDO, 20s + SOCORRO MELENDRES, nb

JR.1.1.5. CELSO RAMORES EFONDO, 30s + LYDIA MORALES, nb

JR.1.1.6. LIBRADA RAMORES EFONDO, 30s + JUAN SEMINIANO, nb
JR.1.1.6.1. AMELIA EFONDO SEMINIANO, 50s + RENATO DELA PUNTA, nb
JR.1.1.6.2. ALFREDO EFONDO SEMINIANO, 50s + MILA DE MATA, nb
JR.1.1.6.3. MYRNA EFONDO SEMINIANO, 50s + LEONARDO GADIL, nb
JR.1.1.6.4. NENITA EFONDO SEMINIANO, 50s + BOBOY PIOQUINTO, nb
JR.1.1.6.5. ARNEL EFONDO SEMINIANO, 60s + THELMA, nb
JR.1.1.6.6. ANTONIO EFONDO SEMINIANO, 60s
JR.1.1.6.7. LOIDA EFONDO SEMINIANO, 60s + MR. ILAGAN, nb
JR.1.1.6.8. SUSAN EFONDO SEMINIANO, 60s + ARNEL GALLARDO, nb
JR.1.1.6.9. CARLITO EFONDO SEMINIANO, 70s
JR.1.1.6.10. SONIA EFONDO SEMINIANO, 70s + MR. CARIAGA, nb
JR.1.1.6.11. LANIE EFONDO SEMINIANO, 70s + JERRY SARICAL, nb

JR.1.1.7. GUIDE RAMORES EFONDO, 30s
JR.1.1.8.. CLAUDIO RAMORES EFONDO, 30s, RIP + SALVACION CORTEZ, nb
JR.1.1.8.1. ANA CORTEZ EFONDO, 50s + HUSBAND, nb
JR.1.1.8.1.1. SCOTT EFONDO-SURNAME, 70s

JR.1.1.8.2. IMELDA CORTEZ EFONDO, 50s + LEONARDO ABRIO, nb
JR.1.1.8.2.1. PATRICIA ANN EFONDO ABRIO, 70s
JR.1.1.8.2.2. LYZA EFONDO ABRIO, 70s
JR.1.1.8.2.3. ANGELA EFONDO ABRIO, 70s
JR.1.1.8.2.4. CASSANDRA EFONDO ABRIO, 80s
JR.1.1.8.3. ARIEL CORTEZ EFONDO, 50s + LOIDA MAESA, nb

JR.1.1.8.4. MANUEL CORTEZ EFONDO, 50s
JR.1.1.8.5. VIOLETA CORTEZ EFONDO, 60s
JR.1.1.8.6. VICTOR CORTEZ EFONDO, 60s
JR.1.1.8.7. ALEX CORTEZ EFONDO, 60s
JR.1.1.8.8. OSCAR CORTEZ EFONDO, 60s
JR.1.1.8.9. CARMELA CORTEZ EFONDO, 70s
JR.1.1.8.10. ALLAN CORTEZ EFONDO, 70s

JR.1.1.9. LYDIA RAMORES EFONDO, 40s + CESAR UBANA, nb
JR.1.1.9.1. MAGGI EFONDO UBANA, 60s
JR.1.1.9.2. GEMMA EFONDO UBANA, 60s
JR.1.1.9.3. JASMIN EFONDO UBANA, 60s + CESARIO CABINGAN, nb

JR.1.2. ANASTACIA MAGANA RAMORES, 1900s + ALEJANDRO OLTAZAR, nb

JR.1.2.1. DIOSDADA RAMORES OLTAZAR, 20s
JR.1.2.2. NAZARIO RAMORES OLTAZAR, 20s

JR.1.3. VICENTE MAGANA RAMORES, 1900s + CEFERINA CLACIO, nb

JR.1.3.1. MARCIANO CLACIO RAMORES, 20s + SALVACION AMADO, nb
JR.1.3.1.1. CARLOS AMADO RAMORES, 40s + ROSITA DELOS SANTOS, nb
JR.1.3.1.1.1. ANALYN DELOSSANTOS RAMORES, 60s + FREDERICK BALTAZAR, nb

JR.1.3.1.2. MARCIANO AMADO RAMORES JR, 40s
JR.1.3.1.3. MARY JANE AMADO RAMORES, 40s

JR.1.3.2. VALENTIN CLACIO RAMORES, 20s + ANECITA ORENDAIN, nb
JR.1.3.2.1. ERLINDA ORENDAIN RAMORES, 40s + ANTONIO CLABE, nb
JR.1.3.2.1.1 GLENN RAMORES CLABE, 60s

JR.1.3.2.2. EMILIA ORENDAIN RAMORES, 40s + ELISEO LAVARRO, nb
JR.1.3.2.2.1. ELENA RAMORES LAVARRO, 60s + EDWIN ANDAYA, nb

JR.1.3.2.2.2. LORNA RAMORES LAVARRO, 60s + DENNIS, nb
JR.1.3.2.2.2.1. JAY-AR LAVARRO-SURNAME, 80s

JR.1.3.2.2.3. MARICEL RAMORES LAVARRO, 60s
JR.1.2.2.2.4. ANALISA RAMORES LAVARRO, 70s
JR.1.2.2.2.5. MYRA RAMORES LAVARRO, 70s
JR.1.3.2.2.6. RIC RAMORES LAVARRO, 70s

JR.1.3.2.3. ELY ORENDAIN RAMORES, 40s + ROMEO PENAREDONDO, nb
JR.1.3.2.4. ELSA ORENDAIN RAMORES, 50s + CONRADO FERNANDEZ, nb
JR.1.3.2.4.1. ANALYN RAMORES FERNANDEZ, 70s

JR.1.3.2.5. REYNALDO ORENDAIN RAMORES, 50s + GINA, nb
JR.1.3.2.6. ANTONIO ORENDAIN RAMORES, 50s + EVELYN DE GUZMAN, nb
JR.1.3.2.6.1. LYZEL DEGUZMAN RAMORES, 70s
JR.1.3.2.6.2. JULYSES DEGUZMAN RAMORES, 70s
JR.1.3.2.6.3. BABYLYN DEGUZMAN RAMORES, 70s
JR.1.3.2.6.4. ANTONIO DEGUZMAN RAMORES JR, 80s

JR.1.3.3. GUADALUPE CLACIO RAMORES, 20s + RUFINO EGAR, nb
JR.1.3.3.1. ARNULFO RAMORES EGAR, 40s + YOLANDA GAMIER, nb
JR.1.3.3.1.1. JOANN GAMIER EGAR, 60s + ARVIN, nb
JR.1.3.3.1.2. MICHAEL GAMIER EGAR, 60s + GELYN, nb
JR.1.3.3.1.2.1. JASON GELYN EGAR, 80s

JR.1.3.3.2. MARIO RAMORES EGAR, 40s + ANITA RAMOS, nb
JR.1.3.3.2.1. MARVIN RAMOS EGAR, 60s
JR.1.3.3.2.2. MARY ANN RAMOS EGAR, 60s

JR.1.3.3.3. BELLA RAMORES EGAR, 40s + ANOTNIO RAMOS, nb
JR.1.3.3.3.1. JOHN ERIC EGAR RAMOS, 60s

JR.1.3.3.4. LORNA RAMORES EGAR, 40s + CARLO VANAN, nb
JR.1.3.3.4.1. GENNALYN EGAR VANAN, 60s
JR.1.3.3.4.2. HONEYLET EGAR VANAN, 60s

Publisher - Tatay Jobo Elizes

JR.1.3.3.4.3. JOHN CARLO EGAR VANAN, 60s
JR.1.3.3.4.4. MARK ANTHONY EGAR VANAN, 70s

JR.1.3.3.5. EDWIN RAMORES EGAR, 50s + MARISSA MAGANA, nb
JR.1.3.3.5.1. FRANCIS MAGANA EGAR, 70s
JR.1.3.3.5.2. KRISTINE MAGANA EGAR, 70s
JR.1.3.3.5.3. ROXANIE MAGANA EGAR, 70s
JR.1.3.3.5.4. EDMAR MAGANA EGAR, 70s
JR.1.3.3.5.5. NERISSA MAGANA EGAR, 80s
JR.1.3.3.5.6. JOHN RICKY MAGANA EGAR, 80s
JR.1.3.3.5.7. JUVITA MAGANA EGAR, 80s

JR.1.3.3.6. NORA RAMORES EGAR, 50s + ANOTNIO CALAG, nb
JR.1.3.3.6.1. ANTONETTE EGAR CALAG, 70s
JR.1.3.3.6.2. ANGELYN EGAR CALAG, 70s

JR.1.3.3.7. RUFINO RAMORES EGAR JR, 50s + JENNETTE JEREZ, nb
JR.1.3.3.7.1. JHUNETTE JEREZ EGAR, 70s
JR.1.3.3.7.2. MELANIE JEREZ EGAR, 70s
JR.1.3.3.8. DOLORES RAMORES EGAR, 50s

JR.1.3.3.9. MARCIAL RAMORES EGAR, 60s - NANETTE SACRIZ, nb
JR.1.3.3.9.1. MANETE SACRIZ EGAR, 80s
JR.1.3.3.9.2. MARICAL SACRIZ EGAR, 80s
JR.1.3.3.9.3. MARLON SACRIZ EGAR, 80s

JR.1.3.4. ANGELINA CLACIO RAMORES, 30s + DOMINGO SANCHEZ, nb
JR.1.3.4.1. DANUEL RAMORES SANCHEZ, 50s + GENNALYN RANA, nb
JR.1.3.4.2. DIOSDADO RAMORES SANCHEZ, 50s
JR.1.3.4.3. DOMINGO RAMORES SANCHEZ JR, 50s + NENENG, nb

JR.1.3.5. PATROCINIO CLACIO RAMORES, 30s

JR.1.3.6. DOMINGO CLACIO RAMORES, 30s + ROSITA MAESA, nb
JR.1.3.6.1. ARIEL MAESA RAMORES, 50s + VIOLETA, nb
JR.1.3.6.2. BELINDA MAESA RAMORES, 50s
JR.1.3.6.3. CARLITO MAESA RAMORES, 50s
JR.1.3.6.4. DOMINGO MAESA RAMORES JR, 50s

JR.1.3.6.5. EMMANUEL MAESA RAMORES, 60s
JR.1.3.6.6. FLERIDA MAESA RAMORES, 60s
JR.1.3.6.7. HEIDI MAESA RAMORES, 60s

JR.1.3.7. MANUEL CLACIO RAMORES, 30s
JR.1.3.8. ROGELIO CLACIO RAMORES, 40s + FELY, nb
JR.1.3.9. VICENTE CLACIO RAMORES JR, 40s + SONIA BRAGA, nb

JR.1.4. ANDREA MAGANA RAMORES, 20s + FIDEL FREYRA(nb)

JR.1.4.1. MODESTA RAMORES FREYRA, 40s
JR.1.4.2. ROSARIO RAMORES FREYRA, 40s + HILARIO ABRERA, nb
JR.1.4.2.1. DOMINGO FREYRA ABRERA, 60s + YOLLY SAVILLA, nb
JR.1.4.2.1.1. LORNA SAVILLA ABRERA, 80s + NEIL BALANE, nb
JR.1.4.2.1.2. DENNIS SAVILLA ABRERA, 80s
JR.1.4.2.1.3. LIZA SAVILLA ABRERA, 80s

JR.1.4.2.2. MIGUEL FREYRA ABRERA, 60s + WIFE MAGO, nb
JR.1.4.2.3. ALBERTO FREYRA ABRERA, 60s + YOLANDA VILLANUEVA, nb
JR.1.4.2.3.1. LINDA VILLANUEVA ABRERA, 80s
JR.1.4.2.3.2. HELEN VILLANUEVA ABRERA, 80s
JR.1.4.2.3.3. ARLENE VILLANUEVA ABRERA, 80s
JR.1.4.2.3.4. RICHARD VILLANUEVA ABRERA, 90s

JR.1.4.2.4. EFREN FREYRA ABRERA, 70s + ERLINDA VILLA, nb
JR.1.4.2.5. LILIA FREYRA ABRERA, 70s + NESTOR, nb
JR.1.4.2.5.1. SHIELA ABRERA-SURNAME, 90s
JR.1.4.2.6. EDWIN FREYRA ABRERA, 70s + JOVITA(nb)
JR.1.4.2.7. EDGARDO FREYRA ABRERA, 80s

JR.1.4.3. ANACITA RAMORES FREYRA, 40s
JR.1.4.4. MARIA RAMORES FREYRA, 40s + PEDRO SAYNO, nb
JR.1.4.5. NOE RAMORES FREYRA, 50s + EDUVIGES EFONDO, nb
JR.1.4.6. ZENAIDA RAMORES FREYRA, 50s + FERMIN BAYNOSA, nb
JR.1.4.7. EDUARDO RAMORES FREYRA, 50s + ANITA MAGO, nb
JR.1.4.8. LUISA RAMORES FREYRA, 60s + RUBEN, nb

JR.1.4.9. ERNESTO RAMORES FREYRA, 60s

JR.1.5. BENIGNO BARCE RAMORES, 30s + ANGELA EFA, nb

JR.1.5.1. EFREN EFA RAMORES, 50s + NORMA MISLANA, nb
JR.1.5.2. CONSUELO EFA RAMORES, 50s + SANTIAGO GACHE, nb
JR.1.5.2.1. JEANETTE RAMORES GACHE, 70s
JR.1.5.2.2. SANTIAGO RAMORES GACHE JR, 70s
JR.1.5.2.3. SHERYL RAMORES GACHE, 70s + DENNIS MAGO, nb
JR.1.5.2.4. SYBEL RAMORES GACHE, 80s
JR.1.5.3. DELFIN EFA RAMORES, 50s + GLORIA ASIS, nb
JR.1.5.3.1. EDGAL ASIS RAMORES, 70s + JOANA, nb
JR.1.5.3.1.1. ANGELO JOANA RAMORES, 90s
JR.1.5.3.1.2. MAYA JOANA RAMORES, 90s

JR.1.5.3.2. DELFIN ASIS RAMORES JR, 70s
JR.1.5.3.3. FRITZEE ASIS RAMORES, 70s
JR.1.5.3.4. LESLIE ASIS RAMORES, 70s

JR.1.5.4. CELSO EFA RAMORES, 60s + AMABLE EFA, nb
JR.1.5.4.1. ANGELITA EFA RAMORES, 80s + ROBERTO PUZON, nb
JR.1.5.4.1.1. ROBERTO RAMORES PUZON JR, 90s
JR.1.5.4.1.2. ANGELO RAMORES PUZON, 90s

JR.1.5.4.2. NELSON EFA RAMORES, 80s + LENY, nb
JR.1.5.4.3. BITUIN EFA RAMORES, 80s

JR.1.5.5. GIL EFA RAMORES, 60s + VIOLETA ABINA, nb
JR.1.5.5.1. GILETA ABINA RAMORES, 80s
JR.1.5.5.2. DERBY ABINA RAMORES, 80s
JR.1.5.5.3. MELODY ABINA RAMORES, 80s

JR.1.5.6. SONIA EFA RAMORES, 60s + GAUDENCIO MAGO, nb
JR.1.5.6.1. ANGELO RAMORES MAGO, 80s
JR.1.5.6.2. AL RAMORES MAGO, 80s
JR.1.5.6.3. REY RAMORES MAGO, 80s

JR.1.6. ROMANA BARCE RAMORES, 30s + JUAN OLIVA, nb

Publisher - Tatay Jobo Elizes

JR.1.6.1. REMEDIOS RAMORES OLIVA, 50s + RIZALINO SEVILLA, nb
JR.1.6.2. CAMILO RAMORES OLIVA, 50s
JR.1.6.3. LUTGARDA RAMORES OLIVA, 50s

JR.2. EUSEBIO JAMITO RAMORES, 1890s + TOMASA BARLETA, nb

JR.2.1. DOMINGA BARLETA RAMORES, 10s + CLETO AGUILAR, nb

JR.2.1.1. GREGORIO RAMORES AGUILAR, 30s + LILIA PIXCIO, nb
JR.2.1.1.1. AIDA PIXCIO AGUILAR, 50s
JR.2.1.1.2. BENHUR PIXCIO AGUILAR, 50s + NELY PLAZA, nb
JR.2.1.1.2.1. CASEY JANE PLAZA AGUILAR, 70s
JR.2.1.1.2.2. ERLY GRACE PLAZA AGUILAR, 70s

JR.2.1.1.3. CLARICE PIXCIO AGUILAR, 50s + BUDDY PIEZA, nb
JR.2.1.1.3.1. BROD MICHAEL AGUILAR PIEZA, 70s

JR.2.1.1.4. GREGORIO PIXCIO AGUILAR JR, 60s + MARICON LOPEZ, nb
JR.2.1.1.5. NIEL PIXCIO AGUILAR, 60s + HAZEL GRACE ZANTUA, nb
JR.2.1.1.5.1. JOHN CHRISTOPHER ZANTUA AGUILAR, 80s

JR.2.1.2. CLETO RAMORES AGUILAR JR, 30s + NIEVES LASCANO, nb
JR.2.1.2.1. ACHILLES LASCANO AGUILAR, 50s + EVANGELINE, nb
JR.2.1.2.1.1. ACHILINE EVANGELINE AGUILAR, 70s
JR.2.1.2.1.2. SHIEVA EVANGELINE AGUILAR, 70s
JR.2.1.2.1.3. DENMARK EVANGELINE AGUILAR, 70s

JR.2.1.2.2. RAMON LASCANO AGUILAR, 50s + ANNIE, nb
JR.2.1.2.2.1. RYAN ANNIE AGUILAR, 70s
JR.2.1.2.2.2. RAMON ANNIE AGUILAR JR, 70s
JR.2.1.2.2.3. RONALD ANNIE AGUILAR, 70s
JR.2.1.2.3. ALEJO LASCANO AGUILAR, 50s + ANALYN ENCINA, nb
JR.2.1.2.3.1. ANJO ENCINA AGUILAR, 70s
JR.2.1.2.3.2. JOAN ENCINA AGUILAR, 70s

Publisher - Tatay Jobo Elizes

JR.2.1.2.3.3. JONA MAY ENCINA AGUILAR, 70s

JR.2.1.2.4. ROMMEL LASCANO AGUILAR, 50s
JR.2.1.2.5. MARCO LASCANO AGUILAR, 60s
JR.2.1.2.6. LOUIE LASCANO AGUILAR, 60s + AILEEN DECENA, nb
JR.2.1.2.6.1. CLETO DECENA AGUILAR III, 80s
JR.2.1.2.6.2. CLAIRE DECENA AGUILAR, 80s

JR.2.1.3. BELEN RAMORES AGUILAR, 30s + CARMELITO BUAN, nb

(Special Note: Belen Ramores Aguilar Buan is caretaker of the original list of this Jamito Family Tree, typewritten in several pages of bond paper, a complete set and pasted in a large map showing the complete chart. She gave me a copy. Belen and I were classmates and finished Elementary together in 1947 in Talisay - Tatay Jobo Elizes, Publisher.)

JR.2.1.3.1. AIMON AGUILAR BUAN, 50s + EVA FRANCISCO, nb
JR.2.1.3.1.1. EUDES AIMON FRANCISCO BUAN, 70s

JR.2.1.3.2. LAURENTI AGUILAR BUAN, 50s + EXCELSA-DINDIN FILIO, nb
JR.2.1.3.2.1. JACQUELINE MAY FILIO BUAN, 70s
JR.2.1.3.2.2. NICHOLO KYLE FILIO BUAN, 70s

JR.2.1.3.3. CRESCENTE AGUILAR BUAN, 50s + ASHIELA BUAN, nb
JR.2.1.3.4. ADELWISA AGUILAR BUAN, 60s

JR.2.1.4. CORAZON RAMORES AGUILAR, 40s + RENATO SANTOS, nb
JR.2.1.4.1. JONAS AGUILAR SANTOS, 60s + CHARINA SANTOS, nb
JR.2.1.4.1.1. JANUS JEMUEL SANTOS, 80s
JR.2.1.4.1.2. JAN-JAN SANTOS, 80s
JR.2.1.4.1.3. CAMILLE SANTOS, 80s
JR.2.1.4.1.4. JOHANS SANTOS, 90s

JR.2.1.4.2. FROILAN AGUILAR SANTOS, 60s + OFELIA, nb
JR.2.1.4.2.1. SHIMBERLY SANTOS, 80s
JR.2.1.4.2.2. JESSRY SANTOS, 80s

JR.2.1.4.3. RENATO AGUILAR SANTOS JR, 60s + RHEA, nb

JR.2.1.4.3.1. RENEA SANTOS, 80s
JR.2.1.4.3.2. JL SANTOS, 80s
JR.2.1.4.4. JASON AGUILAR SANTOS, 70s
JR.2.1.4.5. FARON AGUILAR SANTOS, 70s + ROSALIE PASCUA, nb
JR.2.1.4.5.1. FARAON PASCUA SANTOS, 90s
JR.2.1.4.6. DEO VOLENTE AGUILAR SANTOS, 70s

JR.2.1.5. HUGO RAMORES AGUILAR, 40s + MARGOTT DIAZ, nb
JR.2.1.5.1. ARIEL DIAZ AGUILAR, 60s

JR.2.1.6. JOSE RAMORES AGUILAR, 40s + CRISELDA DURANTE, nb
JR.2.1.6.1. JOCELYN DURANTE AGUILAR, 60s

JR.2.2. OLIMPIO BARLETA RAMORES, 10s + FELIPA MAGANA, nb

JR.2.2.1. AURORA MAGANA RAMORES, 30s + FELIPE YANTO, nb
JR.2.2.1.1. FE RAMORES YANTO, 50s
JR.2.2.1.2. EDEN RAMORES YANTO, 50s
JR.2.2.1.3. MERCY RAMORES YANTO, 50s
JR.2.2.1.4. FELIPE RAMORES YANTO JR, 60s
JR.2.2.1.5. ALFREDO RAMORES YANTO, 60s

JR.2.2.2. BEMJAMIN MAGANA RAMORES, 30s + PILAR CAMA, nb
JR.2.2.2.1. VIRGINIA CAMA RAMORES, 50s
JR.2.2.2.2. 2ND CAMA RAMORES, 50s
JR.2.2.2.3. 3RD CAMA RAMORES, 50s

JR.2.2.3. EUSEBIO MAGANA RAMORES, 30s + AURELIA COLAN, nb
JR.2.2.3.1. ELSA COLAN RAMORES, 50s
JR.2.2.3.2. EFREN COLAN RAMORES, 50s
JR.2.2.3.3. ESTELA COLAN RAMORES, 50s
JR.2.2.3.4. CANDELARIA COLAN RAMORES, 60s
JR.2.2.3.5. ELISA COLAN RAMORES, 60s
JR.2.2.3.6. EXEQUIEL COLAN RAMORES, 60s
JR.2.2.3.7. ENRIQUE COLAN RAMORES, 70s
JR.2.2.3.8. EDWIN COLAN RAMORES, 70s

Publisher - Tatay Jobo Elizes

JR.2.2.4. PAZ MAGANA RAMORES, 40s + ROGELIO CACHO, nb
JR.2.2.4.1. RODEL RAMORES CACHO, 60s
JR.2.2.4.2. ROWEL RAMORES CACHO, 60s
JR.2.2.4.3. RAUL RAMORES CACHO, 60s
JR.2.2.4.4. ROSALYN RAMORES CACHO, 70s
JR.2.2.4.5. ROWENA RAMORES CACHO, 70s
JR.2.2.4.6. RAMIL RAMORES CACHO, 70s
JR.2.2.4.7. RUBNEN RAMORES CACHO, 80s
JR.2.2.4.8. RONALD RAMORES CACHO, 80s
JR.2.2.4.9. ROBELYN RAMORES CACHO, 80s

JR.2.3. QUINTIN BARLETA RAMORES, 10s, RIP

JR.2.4. VICTORIA BARLETA RAMORES, 20s + FRANCISCO AREVALO, nb

JR.2.4.1. ERNESTO RAMORES AREVALO, 40s + EXPECTACION, nb
JR.2.4.1.1. EXCELSA AREVALO, 60s + HUSBAND, nb
JR.2.4.1.1.1. ALBERT AREVALO-SURNAME, 80s
JR.2.4.1.1.2. RONALD AREVALO-SURNAME, 80s
JR.2.4.1.1.3. GARNET AREVALO-SURNAME, 80s

JR.2.4.1.2. EMILY AREVALO, 60s + CARMELO AVELINIA, nb
JR.2.4.1.2.1. AIREEN AREVALO AVELINIA, 80s
JR.2.4.1.2.2. MARY AREVALO ANN AVELINIA, 80s
JR.2.4.1.2.3. 3RD AREVALO AVELINIA, 80s

JR.2.4.1.3. BELEN AREVALO, 60s + ELMER AVELINIA, nb
JR.2.4.1.3.1. 1ST AREVALO AVELINIA, 80s
JR.2.4.1.3.2. 2ND AREVALO AVELINIA, 80s

JR.2.4.1.4. ELSA AREVALO, 70s
JR.2.4.1.5. EDEN AREVALO, 70s + DANILO MARTILLAN, nb

JR.2.4.1.6. ERMA AREVALO, 70s + ALBERT BONGALON, nb
JR.2.4.1.6.1. HAROLD AREVALO BONGALON, 90s
JR.2.4.1.6.2. 2ND AREVALO BONGALON, 90s

JR.2.4.1.7. ESTELITA AREVALO, 80s
JR.2.4.1.8. ESTELA AREVALO, 80s + LOUIE JOVAN, nb
JR.2.4.1.9. ERNESTO AREVALO JR, 80s

JR.2.4.2. MAGNO RAMORES AREVALO, 40s + NORMA CUBINAR, nb
JR.2.4.2.1. ROSAURO CUBINAR AREVALO, 60s

JR.2.4.3. ROMEO RAMORES AREVALO, 40s + LETICIA BRAZOS, nb
JR.2.4.3.1. REXY BRAZOS AREVALO, 60s + ZALDY CALLADA, nb
JR.2.4.3.1.1. ARJAY CALLADA AREVALO, 80s
JR.2.4.3.1.2. ELOISA MARIE CALLADA AREVALO, 80s
JR.2.4.3.1.3. MARK VINCENT CALLADA AREVALO, 80s
JR.2.4.3.1.4. KHEVIN JOY CALLADA AREVALO, 90s
JR.2.4.3.1.5. MARIA KRIZZEL CALLADA AREVALO, 90s

JR.2.4.3.2. REGINA BRAZOS AREVALO, 60s + JUANITO CUEVO, nb
JR.2.4.3.2.1. JUANA ROSE AREVALO CUEVO, 80s
JR.2.4.3.2.2. JONABEL AREVALO CUEVO, 80s
JR.2.4.3.2.3. JESSICA AREVALO CUEVO, 80s
JR.2.4.3.2.4. JANINE CLAUDETTE AREVALO CUEVO, 90s
JR.2.4.3.2.5. JULIE MARIE AREVALO CUEVO, 90s

JR.2.4.3.3. ROBINA BRAZOS AREVALO, 60s + LUIS CUADERES, nb
JR.2.4.3.3.1. KRIS MARIE JOYCE AREVALO CUADERES, 80s
JR.2.4.3.3.2. KENNETH AREVALO CUADERES, 80s

JR.2.4.3.4. REBECCA BRAZOS AREVALO, 70s + RODEL GARCIA, nb
JR.2.4.3.4.1. CINDY AREVALO GARCIA, 90s
JR.2.4.3.4.2. JOHN PATRICK AREVALO GARCIA, 90s
JR.2.4.3.4.3. KRISTINE MAY AREVALO GARCIA, 90s
JR.2.4.3.4.4. JOHN RABI AREVALO GARCIA, 90s

JR.2.4.3.5. ROMMEL BRAZOS AREVALO, 70s + ANGELINA ARAGON, nb
JR.2.4.3.5.1. MARK JOHNZEN ARAGON AREVALO, 90s

JR.2.4.3.6. ROSALIE BRAZOS AREVALO, 70s + SERAFIN ABUYO, nb
JR.2.4.3.6.1. 1ST. AREVALO ABUYO, 90s

Publisher - Tatay Jobo Elizes

JR.2.4.4. ROGELIO RAMORES AREVALO, 40s + LILIA IBIS, nb
JR.2.4.4.1. ARNOLD IBIS AREVALO, 60s + ZAIDA CALUBAYAN, nb
JR.2.4.4.1.1. AARON CALUBAYAN AREVALO, 80s
JR.2.4.4.1.2. AMIEL CALUBAYAN AREVALO, 80s
JR.2.4.4.1.3. ARIAN CALUBAYAN AREVALO, 80s

JR.2.4.4.2. ALLAN IBIS AREVALO, 60s + SARAH BAAY, nb
JR.2.4.4.2.1. LANIE BAAY AREVALO, 80s

JR.2.4.4.3. SHIRLEY IBIS AREVALO, 60s + DENNIS ABITAL, nb
JR.2.4.4.3.1. JOVELYN AREVALO ABITAL, 80s
JR.2.4.4.3.2. SHIRLYDEN AREVALO ABITAL, 80s
JR.2.4.4.3.3. DANICA AREVALO ABITAL, 80s
JR.2.4.4.4. JOSIE IBIS AREVALO, 60s + HERMINIO BAROSA, nb
JR.2.4.4.4.1. HANNAH GWEN AREVALO BAROSA, 80s
JR.2.4.4.4.2. HERNAN AREVALO BAROSA, 80s
JR.2.4.4.4.3. KAREN AREVALO BAROSA, 80s

JR.2.4.4.5. NELSON IBIS AREVALO, 70s + SUSAN GACHO, nb
JR.2.4.4.5.1. KARLENEN GACHO AREVALO, 90s
JR.2.4.4.6. JEANETTE IBIS AREVALO, 70s
JR.2.4.4.7. CLARISA IBIS AREVALO, 70s + ROY ZANTUA, nb

JR.2.4.5. FRANCISCO RAMORES AREVALO JR, 40s + LENIDA, nb
JR.2.4.5.1. DENNISE LENIDA AREVALO, 60s
JR.2.4.5.2. GINA LENIDA AREVALO, 60s
JR.2.4.5.3. VIVIAN LENIDA AREVALO, 60s
JR.2.4.5.4. ALVIN LENIDA AREVALO, 60s, RIP
JR.2.4.5.5. JOJO LENIDA AREVALO, 70s, RIP
JR.2.4.5.6. MYRIAM LENIDA AREVALO, 70s
JR.2.4.5.7. BARTOLOME LENIDA AREVALO, 70s
JR.2.4.5.8. FRANCIS LENIDA AREVALO, 70s
JR.2.4.5.9. FATIMA LENIDA AREVALO, 80s
JR.2.4.5.10. GILBERT LENIDA AREVALO, 80s
JR.2.4.5.11. JEREMY LENIDA AREVALO, 80s
JR.2.4.5.12. JOSHWA LENIDA AREVALO, 80s

Publisher - Tatay Jobo Elizes

JR.2.4.6. ELISA RAMORES AREVALO, 40s + ALFREDO GASIS, nb
JR.2.4.6.1. RUEL AREVALO GASIS, 60s + JENNY, nb
JR.2.4.6.1.1. MARK GIL GASIS, 80s
JR.2.4.6.1.2. JULIE ANN GASIS, 80s
JR.2.4.6.1.3. ANA GAIL GASIS, 80s
JR.2.4.6.1.4. ABEGAIL GASIS, 90s
JR.2.4.6.1.5. RUEL GASIS JR, 90s

JR.2.4.6.2. ROLANDO AREVALO GASIS, 60s

JR.2.4.7. EMELITA RAMORES AREVALO, 50s + CARLITO DANIEL, nb
JR.2.4.7.1. CARMELITA AREVALO DANIEL, 70s + RODEL WABON, nb
JR.2.4.7.1.1. MARY ROSE DANIEL WABON, 90s
JR.2.4.7.1.2. CJ DANIEL WABON, 90s

JR.2.4.7.2. CARMELA AREVALO DANIEL, 70S + ARMANDO DELA CRUZ, nb
JR.2.4.7.2.1. ARNALYN DANIEL DELA CRUZ, 90s
JR.2.4.8. ENRIQUE RAMORES AREVALO, 50s

JR.3. MIGUEL JAMITO RAMORES, 10s + ROSARIO BARON, nb

JR.3.1. SIMEON B. RAMORES, 30s + MARIA YANESA, nb

JR.3.1.1. JOSE YANESA RAMORES, 50s
JR.3.1.2. JESUS YANESA RAMORES, 50s
JR.3.1.3. JUANITO YANESA RAMORES, 50s
JR.3.1.4. FRANCISCA YANESA RAMORES, 60s
JR.3.1.5. WILFREDO YANESA RAMORES, 60s
JR.3.1.6. AUGUSTO YANESA RAMORES, 60s
JR.3.1.7. DOLORES YANESA RAMORES, 70s
JR.3.1.8. SIMEON YANESA RAMORES, 70s

JR.3.2. ISABEL BARON RAMORES, 30s + MAMERTO ZANTUA, nb

JR.3.2.1. ROLANDO RAMORES ZANTUA, 50s
JR.3.2.2. ROBERTO RAMORES ZANTUA, 50s, RIP
JR.3.2.3. ARTEMIO RAMORES ZANTUA, 50s

JR.3.2.4. CORAZON RAMORES ZANTUA, 60s + CARMELO YBAROLA, nb
JR.3.2.4.1. CARMELO ZANTUA YBAROLA JR, 80s
JR.3.2.4.2. RAYMOND ZANTUA YBAROLA, 80s

JR.3.2.5. EMERLINA RAMORES ZANTUA, 60s + HUSBAND, nb
JR.3.2.5.1. RANJIT ZANTUA-SURNAME, 80s
JR.3.2.5.2. SARJIT ZANTUA-SURNAME, 80s
JR.3.2.5.3. HARJIT ZANTUA-SURNAME. 80s
JR.3.2.5.4. SETHVENDER ZANTUA-SURNAME. 90s

JR.3.2.6. DOLORES RAMORES ZANTUA, 60s

JR.3.2.7. MA. CRISTINA RAMORES ZANTUA, 70s + JAIME AREVALO, nb
JR.3.2.7.1. DIANA ALEA ZANTUA AREVALO, 90s
JR.3.2.7.2. JUDE ANTHONY ZANTUA AREVALO, 90s

JR.3.3. JOSE BARON RAMORES, 20s, RIP

JR.3.4. JUANA B. RAMORES, 20s + ELIGIO TEODORO, nb
JR.3.4.1. FLORA RAMORES TEODORO, 40s + JOSE FLORENTES, nb
JR.3.4.1.1. RUDY TEODORO FLORENTES, 60s + AMPARO IBANA, nb
JR.3.4.1.1.1. JOVEN IBANA FLORENTES, 80s + CHARITO ORTIZ, nb
JR.3.4.1.1.1.1. JOHN KEVIN ORTIZ FLORENTES, 00s
JR.3.4.1.1.1.2. SHAMINE ORTIZ FLORENTES, 00s
JR.3.4.1.1.2. RONNIE IBANA FLORENTES, 80s
JR.3.4.1.1.3. RUDY IBANA FLORENTES JR, 80S

JR.3.4.1.2. JULITA TEODORO FLORENTES, 60s + ALEJANDRO GOMEZ, nb
JR.3.4.1.2.1. VILMA FLORENTES GOMEZ, 80s + FREDDIE SALIDONG, nb
JR.3.4.1.2.1.1. ROBERT GOMEZ SALIDONG, 00s
JR.3.4.1.2.1.2. RAUL GOMEZ SALIDONG, 00s
JR.3.4.1.2.1.3. FREDDIE GOMEZ SALIDONG JR, 00s

JR.3.4.1.2.1.4. DELMA GOMEZ SALIDONG, 00s

JR.3.4.1.2.2. SALLY FLORENTES GOMEZ, 80s + WILLY ADATING, nb
JR.3.4.1.2.2.1. ROLANDO GOMEZ ADATING, 00s
JR.3.4.1.2.2.2. NENENG GOMEZ ADATING, 00s

JR.3.4.1.2.3. JUNE FLORENTES GOMEZ, 80s
JR.3.4.1.2.4. CESAR FLORENTES GOMEZ, 80s + TERESITA PENARANDA, nb
JR.3.4.1.2.4.1. CRISTINA PENARANDA GOMEZ, 00s
JR.3.4.1.2.4.2. BENHUR PENARANDA GOMEZ, 00s
JR.3.4.1.2.4.3. BRYAN PENARANDA GOMEZ, 00s
JR.3.4.1.2.4.4. JEAN PENARANDA GOMEZ, 00s

JR.3.4.1.2.5. ANGELINA FLORENTES GOMEZ, 80s + BOBOY GALINAUGA, nb
JR.3.4.1.2.5.1. REGIE GOMEZ GALINAUGA, 00s
JR.3.4.1.2.5.2. RENE GOMEZ GALINAUGA, 00s
JR.3.4.1.2.5.3. CHECHE GOMEZ GALINAUGA, 00s
JR.3.4.1.2.5.4. RR GOMEZ GALINAUGA, 00s

JR.3.4.1.2.6. ENRIQUE FLORENTES GOMEZ, 80s + PAMELA RACHO, nb
JR.3.4.1.2.6.1. JESSRA CHRISTINA RACHO GOMEZ, 00s
JR.3.4.1.2.7. URBANO FLORENTES GOMEZ, 80s, RIP
JR.3.4.1.2.8. CONCEPCION FLORENTES GOMEZ, 80s + MR. SARMIENTO, nb
JR.3.4.1.2.8.1. ADELINA GOMEZ SARMIENTO, 00s
JR.3.4.1.2.8.2. JOSE GOMEZ SARMIENTO, 00s

JR.3.4.1.2.9. MANUEL FLORENTES GOMEZ, 90s

JR.3.5. BEATRIZ BARON RAMORES, 20s + EUGENIO MARIANO, nb

JR.3.5.1. VITO RAMORES MARIANO, 40s + AGRIPINA PLACIDO, nb
JR.3.5.1.1. TERESITA PLACIDO MARIANO, 60s
JR.3.5.1.2. CARLITO PLACIDO MARIANO, 60s

Publisher - Tatay Jobo Elizes

JR.3.5.1.3. NELIA PLACIDO MARIANO, 60s
JR.3.5.1.4. LUZ PLACIDO MARIANO, 70s
JR.3.5.1.5. JANNING PLACIDO MARIANO, 70s
JR.3.5.1.6. VITO PLACIDO MARIANO JR, 70s

JR.3.5.2. EMETERIA RAMORES MARIANO, 40s + CARLOS FREYRA, nb
JR.3.5.2.1. KRISTINE MARIANO FREYRA, 60s
JR.3.5.2.2. ERLINDA MARIANO FREYRA, 60s
JR.3.5.2.3. IMELDA MARIANO FREYRA, 60s
JR.3.5.2.4. MANUEL MARIANO FREYRA, 60s
JR.3.5.2.5. DANTE MARIANO FREYRA, 70s
JR.3.5.2.6. RODEL MARIANO FREYRA, 70s
JR.3.5.2.7. VILMA MARIANO FREYRA, 70s
JR.3.5.2.8. ACELITA MARIANO FREYRA, 70s
JR.3.5.2.9. ARNEL MARIANO FREYRA, 70s

JR.3.5.3. NORA RAMORES MARIANO, 40s + FRANCISCO BAAY, nb
JR.3.5.3.1. DOMINGO MARIANO BAAY, 60s
JR.3.5.3.2. DAISY MARIANO BAAY, 60s
JR.3.5.3.3. BELLA MARIANO BAAY, 60s
JR.3.5.3.4. RODEL MARIANO BAAY, 60s
JR.3.5.3.5. DANTE MARIANO BAAY, 70s
JR.3.5.3.6. NELLIE MARIANO BAAY, 70s
JR.3.5.3.7. ELY MARIANO BAAY, 70s
JR.3.5.3.8. MELCHOR MARIANO BAAY, 70s
JR.3.5.3.9. HENRY MARIANO BAAY, 80s

JR.3.5.4. JULIA RAMORES MARIANO, 40s + AMADO EDORIA, nb
JR.3.5.4.1. VIRGINIA MARIANO EDORIA, 60s + ROMEO DE JESUS, nb
JR.3.5.4.1.1. SHIELA EDORIA DE JESUS, 80s
JR.3.5.4.1.2. SHARON EDORIA DE JESUS, 80s
JR.3.5.4.1.3. ROMEO EDORIA DE JESUS JR, 80s

JR.3.5.4.2. ELMER MARIANO EDORIA, 60s + SUSAN AVELLANA, nb
JR.3.5.4.2.1. AL JEROME AVELLANA EDORIA, 80s
JR.3.5.4.2.2. LEA AVELLANA EDORIA, 80s

JR.3.5.4.3. DELIA MARIANO EDORIA, 60s + JAIME CAMBAY, nb

JR.3.5.4.4. MARILOU MARIANO EDORIA, 60s + DONATO MABEZA, nb
JR.3.5.4.5. DAISY MARIANO EDORIA, 70s + VICENTE, nb
JR.3.5.4.6. ELSA MARIANO EDORIA, 70s + JING, nb
JR.3.5.4.7. AGNES MARIANO EDORIA, 70s + BORJA, nb
JR.3.5.4.8. EDWIN MARIANO EDORIA, 70s + MARILYN ANSUAS, nb

JR.3.5.5. MARIA RAMORES MARIANO, 50s + PABLO LIBRIA, nb
JR.3.5.5.1. ROSARIO MARIANO LIBRIA, 70s + CESAR HERNANDEZ, nb
JR.3.5.5.2. ROMEO MARIANO LIBRIA, 70s
JR.3.5.5.3. JOSE MARIANO LIBRIA, 70s + HELEN CAMACHO, nb
JR.3.5.5.4. ANTONIO MARIANO LIBRIA, 70s + VERONICA, nb
JR.3.5.5.5. VILMA MARIANO LIBRIA, 80s + RODEL ESPANA, nb
JR.3.5.5.6. RAMIL MARIANO LIBRIA, 80s
JR.3.5.5.7. ALLAN MARIANO LIBRIA, 80s
JR.3.5.5.8. ANITA MARIANO LIBRIA, 80s
JR.3.5.5.9. MARIBEL MARIANO LIBRIA, 90s

JR.3.5.6. MARCIANA RAMORES MARIANO, 50s + ALBERTO DE LEON, nb
JR.3.5.6.1. CONCHITA MARIANO DE LEON, 70s + JALET MABEZA, nb
JR.3.5.6.2. ROBIN MARIANO DE LEON, 70s
JR.3.5.6.3. DANTA MARIANO DE LEON, 70s
JR.3.5.6.4. ROMULO MARIANO DE LEON, 70s
JR.3.5.6.5. MYRNA MARIANO DE LEON, 80s
JR.3.5.6.6. LERMA MARIANO DE LEON, 80s
JR.3.5.6.7. ALBERTO MARIANO DE LEON JR, 80s
JR.3.5.6.8. HENRY MARIANO DE LEON, 80s

JR.3.5.7. ZENAIDA RAMORES MARIANO, 50s + ROGELIO DE JESUS, nb
JR.3.5.7.1. AMALIA MARIANO DE JESUS, 70s
JR.3.5.7.2. LEONARDO MARIANO DE JESUS, 70s
JR.3.5.7.3. ZAIDA MARIANO DE JESUS, 70s
JR.3.5.7.4. FE MARIANO DE JESUS, 70s
JR.3.5.7.5. ROSE MARIANO DE JESUS, 80s
JR.3.5.7.6. RIGOR MARIANO DE JESUS, 80s

JR.3.5.8. NATIVIDAD RAMORES MARIANO, 50s + ERNESTO DE LEON, nb
JR.3.5.8.1. NESTOR MARIANO DE LEON, 70s + BELEN PADA, nb

Publisher - Tatay Jobo Elizes

JR.3.5.8.2. RENATO MARIANO DE LEON, 70s + NANING, nb
JR.3.5.8.3. LEONIDA MARIANO DE LEON, 70s + RENE, nb
JR.3.5.8.4. AIDA MARIANO DE LEON, 70s
JR.3.5.8.5. ERNESTO MARIANO DE LEON JR, 80s
JR.3.5.8.6. JULIETA MARIANO DE LEON, 80s + GERRY ABUYO, nb
JR.3.5.8.7. MARILYN MARIANO DE LEON, 80s + ARIEL GADIL, nb
JR.3.5.8.8. ALINA MARIANO DE LEON, 80s
JR.3.5.8.9. MARITES MARIANO DE LEON, 90s

JR.3.5.9. NENITA RAMORES MARIANO, 60s + GIL CAMBRONERO, nb
JR.3.5.9.1. GILDA MARIANO CAMBRONERO, 80s + JOSE CAYABYAB, nb
JR.3.5.9.1.1. JOHN GIL CAMBRONERO CAYABYAB, 00s
JR.3.5.9.1.2. LOTA JAY CAMBRONERO CAYABYAB, 00s
JR.3.5.9.1.3. JESSICA CAMBRONERO CAYABYAB, 00s
JR.3.5.9.1.4. DIANA CAMBRONERO CAYABYAB, 00s

JR.3.5.9.2. NENITO MARIANO CAMBRONERO, 80s + SUSANA GADIL, nb
JR.3.5.9.2.1. NERISSA GADIL CAMBRONERO, 00s
JR.3.5.9.2.2. NELSON GADIL CAMBRONERO, 00s
JR.3.5.9.2.3. BONITA GADIL CAMBRONERO, 00s

JR.3.5.9.3. LUIS MARIANO CAMBRONERO, 80s
JR.3.5.9.4. AIDA MARIANO CAMBRONERO, 80s + ERNESTO ACLADO, nb
JR.3.5.9.4.1. AIMEE DIEL CAMBRONERO ACLADO, 00s
JR.3.5.9.4.2. ERNESTO CAMBRONERO ACLADO JR, 00s

JR.3.5.9.5. AILA MARIANO CAMBRONERO, 80s + CRIS BALDONADO, nb
JR.3.5.9.5.1. CHRISTIAN BALDONADO, 00s
JR.3.5.9.6. ADA MARIANO CAMBRONERO, 90s
JR.3.5.9.7. LOIDA MARIANO CAMBRONERO, 90s

JR.3.5.10. LETICIA RAMORES MARIANO, 60s + JAMIE ESPINAR, nb
JR.3.5.10.1. MELANIE MARIANO ESPINAR, 80s + ALBERTO, nb
JR.3.5.10.2. GLENA MARIANO ESPINAR, 80s
JR.3.5.10.3. ROMMEL MARIANO ESPINAR, 80s
JR.3.5.10.4. MARCOS MARIANO ESPINAR, 90s
JR.3.5.10.5. MARY JANE MARIANO ESPINAR, 90s

SUB - BRANCH
TITO JAMITO +
MARIA RAGILES.
(JRJ - JAMITO - RAGILES, 1910s)

(Tito Jamito is probably a nephew of Patriarch Santiago Jamito. It is interesting to note that his wife Maria Ragiles is recorded sister of Placido Ragiles, husband of Vicenta Jamito, under Branch No. 5 in the Main Jamito Family Tree. This makes them double relatives.)

Publisher - Tatay Jobo Elizes

JRJ.1 GARCIANO RAGILES JAMITO + WIFE
(This might be another big clan but there is No List)

JRJ.2. CANDIDO RAGILES JAMITO, rip 1987 + FELISA ORESCA MATOLA, W1
+ ELENA MENDOZA CASTILLO, W2, rip 2010

JRJ.3. EUGENIA RAGILES JAMITO + HUSBAND SURNAME (List here)

JRJ.3.1. ELENA JAMITO Surname + JOSE MUJAL (No List)

JRJ.4. PABLO RAGILES JAMITO - SINGLE
("KID JAMITO" as DAET BOXER CHAMPION)

~~~~~~~~~~ Family Tree ~~~~~~~~~~

JRJ.2. CANDIDO RAGILES JAMITO, rip 1987 + FELISA ORESCA MATOLA, W1 + ELENA MENDOZA CASTILLO, W2, rip 2010

JRJ.2.1. Esmeraldo Matola Jamito, rip + Milagros Huvalla Villagracia
JRJ.2.1.1. Nemesio Villagracia Jamito + Cecilia Diamante Uriarte
JRJ.2.1.1.1. Lorna Uriarte Jamito + Wilfredo A. Reyes
JRJ.2.1.1.1.1. Lorie Mae Jamito Reyes

JRJ.2.1.1.2. Lucily Uriarte Jamito + Dennis Cantona De La Rosa
JRJ.2.1.1.2.1. Kimberly Jamito Dela Rosa
JRJ.2.1.1.2.2. Cloe Jamito De La Rosa.

JRJ.2.1.1.3. Elmer Uriarte Jamito
JRJ.2.1.1.4. Loradel Uriarte Jamito + Leonardo Cantona Mercurio
JRJ.2.1.1.4.1. Jaycob Jamito Mercurio
JRJ.2.1.1.4.2.Yael Jamito Mercurio
JRJ.2.1.1.5. Mikko Uriarte Jamito

Publisher - Tatay Jobo Elizes

JRJ.2.1.2. Larry Villagracia Jamito Sr.+ Lilian Acosta Abungan
JRJ.2.1.2.1. Lorena Abungan Jamito + husband Joven De Los Santos Neri
JRJ.2.1.2.1.1. Jenica Jamito Neri
JRJ.2.1.2.1.2. John Eric Jamito Neri

JRJ.2.1.2.2. Liezel Abungan Jamito
JRJ.2.1.2.3. Larry Abungan Jamito
JRJ.2.1.2.4. Lea Abungan Jamito
JRJ.2.1.2.5. Leny Abungan Jamito

JRJ.2.1.3. William Villagracia Jamito, rip + Asuncion Almojano Canela, rip
JRJ.2.1.3.1. Jarwin Canela Jamito
JRJ.2.1.3.2. Jelvin Canela Jamito

JRJ.2.1.4. Esterllita Villagracia Jamito + Sadato Umeyo Kataoka
JRJ.2.1.4.1. Sadato Kenji Jamito Kataoka

JRJ.2.1.5. Danilo Villagracia Jamito + Marcelina Quarte Magada
JRJ.2.1.5.1. Jelizer Magada Jamito
JRJ.2.1.5.2. Jeny Magada Jamito+ Carl Christian Maano Dinglasan, rip
JRJ.2.1.5.2.1. Jenica Krista Jamito Dinglasan
JRJ.2.1.5.3. John Lee Magada Jamito
JRJ.2.1.5.4. John Dee Magada Jamito, rip
JRJ.2.1.5.5. Zoe Juriko Magada Jamito

JRJ.2.2. ANACITA MATOLA JAMITO + MARIANO DELOS ANGELES
JRJ.2.2.1. Rogelio Jamito Villafranca + wife Delia Baay
JRJ.2.2.1.1. Dante Baay Villafranca + Elsa Ramos
JRJ.2.2.1.1.1.Noel Ramos Villafranca
JRJ.2.2.1.1.2. Francis Ramos Villafranca
JRJ.2.2.1.1.3. Eric Ramos Villafranca
JRJ.2.2.1.1.4. Mary Joy Ramos Villafranca
JRJ.2.2.1.2. Ramil Baay Villafranca + Nelia Ubana
JRJ.2.2.1.2.1. Ranelyn Ubana Villafranca
JRJ.2.2.1.2.2. Leahmell Ubana Villafranca
JRJ.2.2.1.2.3. Kyte Maria Ubana Villafranca

Publisher - Tatay Jobo Elizes

JRJ.2.2..1.2.4. Darryl Ubana Villafranca
JRJ.2.2.1.2.5. Rizza Jane Ubana Villafranca
JRJ.2.2.1.2.6. Andrie Ubana Villafranca
JRJ.2.2.1.2.7. Janiel Ubana Villafranca

JRJ.2.2.1.3. Ricky Baay Villafranca + Merlita Abordo
JRJ.2.2.1.3.1.Rose May Abordo Villafranca
JRJ.2.2.1.3.2. Raymond Abordo Villafranca
JRJ.2.2.1.3.3. Rhealyn Aburdo Villafranca

JRJ.2.2.1.4. Rogelio Baay Villafranca Jr., rip

JRJ.2.2.1.5. Minerva Baay Villafranca + Jonnie Pabico
JRJ.2.2.1.5.1. Jennelyn Villafrnca Pabico
JRJ.2.2.1.5.2. Kian Jethro Villafranca Pabico

JRJ.2.2.1.6. Rowena Baay Villafranca + Manolo Dela Punta
JRJ.2.2.1.6.1. Jasmine Villafranca Dela Punta

JRJ.2.2.1.7. Ruel Baay Villafrnaca + Marife Molina
JRJ.2.2.1.7.1. Rommel Molina Villafranca
JRJ.2.2.1.7.2. Diana Molina Villafranca
JRJ.2.2.1.7.3.Mary Grace Molina Villafranca

JRJ.2.2.1.8. Myra Baay Villafranca + Bernard Rada
JRJ.2.2.1.8.1.Jhn Lawrence Villafranca Rada

JRJ.2.2.1.9. Rodelia Baay Villafranca + Raymond Yanela
JRJ.2.2.1.9.1.John Ray Villafranca Yanela
JRJ.2B.1.9.2. Kathleen Mae Villafranca Yanela

JRJ.2.2.1.10. Dennis Baay Villafranca

JRJ.2.2.1.11. Jobert Baay Villafranca

JRJ.2.2.2. Felisa Jamito Asido + Husband
JRJ.2.2.2.1. Wilma Delos Angeles Asido + Abraham Bentulan
JRJ.2.2.2.1.1. John Patrick Delos Angeles Bentulan

Publisher - Tatay Jobo Elizes

JRJ.2.2.2.1.2. James Luis Delos Angeles Bentulan

JRJ.2.2.2.2.Rodel Delos Angeles Asido + Alma Policarpio
JRJ.2.2.2.2.1.Adrian Policarpio Asido
JRJ.2.2.2.2.2. Aldrin Policarpio Asido
JRJ.2.2.2.2.3.Madelyn Policarpio Asido
JRJ.2.2.2.2.4. Renz Policarpio Asido
JRJ.2.2.2.2.5. Chammie Policarpio Asido

JRJ.2.2.2.3. Marvin Delos Angeles Asido

JRJ.2.2.3. Angeles Jamito Delos Angeles + Nelia Zafe
JRJ.2.2.3.1. Michelle Zafe Delos Angeles
JRJ.2.2.3.2.Catherine Zafe Delos Angeles

JRJ.2.2.4. Aida Jamito Delos Angeles + Husband Salcedo
JRJ.2.2.4.1.Mary Irish Delos Angels Salcedo + Emman Briguera
JRJ.2.2.4.1.1.Carla Marie Delos Angeles Briguera

JRJ.2.2.4.2.Ronnel Delos Angeles Salcedo + Angela Elep

JRJ.2.2.4.3.Karine Delos Angeles Salcedo + Rey- Ann Cabutotan
JRJ.2.2.4.3.1. Geneva Mae Salcedo Cabutotan
JRJ.2.2.4.3.2. Aida Margareth Salcedo Cabutotan

JRJ.2.2.4.4. Ivy Delos Angeles Salcedo

JRJ.2.2.4.5.Jommel Delos Angeles Salcedo + Antonia Leviste
JRJ.2.2.4.5.1.John Rey Leviste Delos Angeles
JRJ.2.2.4.5.2. Angeline Leviste Delos Angeles

JRJ. 2.2.4.6.Mary Grace Delos Angels Salcedo
JRJ.2.2.4.7.Christian Delos Angeles Salcedo

JRJ.2.2.4.8.Mariano Blas Delos Angeles Salcedo

JRJ.2.2.5.Ruben Jamito Delos Angeles + Elizabeth Verora
JRJ.2.2.5.1. Ruel Verora Delos Angeles

Publisher - Tatay Jobo Elizes

JRJ.2.2.5.2. Ian Verora Delos Angeles
JRJ.2.2.5.3. John Ruiz Verora Delos Angeles

JRJ.2.2.6.Anita Jamito Delos Angeles + Manolo Lorenzana
JRJ.2.2.6.1. Minnie Delos Angeles Lorenzana + Robert Gonzales
JRJ.2.2.6.2. Mylene Delos Angeles Lorenzana
JRJ 2.2.6.3.Manuel Delos Angeles Lorenzana
JRJ.2.2.6.4.Mark Delos Angeles Lorenzana
JRJ.2.2.6.5. Melvin Delos Angeles Lorenzana + Catherine Oseo
JRJ.2.2.6.5.1.Marc Zeus Oseo Lorenzana

JRJ.2.2.6.6. Maureen Delos Angeles Lorenzana
JRJ.2.2.6.7. Mikylla Delos Angeles Lorenzana

JRJ.2.2.7. Joey Boy Jamito Delos Angeles + Ella Tuzon
JRJ.2.2.7.1. Elliot James Tuzon Delos Angeles

JRJ.2.2.8. Joel Jamito Delos Angeles + Jenelie Villanueva
JRJ.2.2.8.1. Joniel Villanueva Delos Angeles
JRJ.2.2.8.2. John Michael Villanueva Delos Angeles
JRJ.2.2.8.3.Justin Jhoy Villanueva Delos Angeles

JRJ. 2.3. AVELINA MATOLA JAMITO, rip +SIXTO BASER JALIMAO SR., rip

JRJ.2.3.1. Nelia Jamito Jalimao - + WILFREDO MAGO ASIS
JRJ.2.3.1.1 ALEXANDER JALIMAO ASIS + ANTONETTE ACIAS
MANZANO
JRJ.2.3.1.1.1. PIA MANZANO ASIS

JRJ.2.3.1.2 . ARISTOTLE JALIMAO ASIS + CHONA DE VELA
JRJ.2.3.1.2.1 JANJAN DE VELA ASIS
JRJ.2.3.1.2.2. BONBON DE VELA ASIS

JRJ.2.3.1.3 ARCHIMEDES JALIMAO ASIS + CHONA GAPOY
JRJ.2.3.1.3.1. JASPER GAPOY ASIS

JRJ.2.3.1.4 . WELNELIZA JALIMAO ASIS + HUSBAND VILLACRUCIS

JRJ.2.3.1.4.1. to follow
JRJ.2.3.1.4.2. to follow
JRJ.2.3.1.4.3. to follow

JRJ.2.3.1.5. ALEJANDRO JALIMAO ASIS

JRJ.2.3.2. LELIA JAMITO JALIMAO + NESTORIO B. ACABADO
JRJ 2.3.2.1. MARITES JALIMAO ACABADO + JULIUS BACOLOD
ENOFRIO
JRJ.2.3.2.1.1. MAY ACABADO ENOFRIO
JRJ.2.3.2.1.2. JOY ACABADO ENOFRIO

JRJ.2.3.2.2. LAILA JALIMAO ACABADO + ROLANDO VALDEZ
VILLAMOR, JR.
JRJ.2.3.2.2.1. LAILANI ACABADO VILLAMOR

JRJ.2.3.2.3 . ARTHUR JALIMAO ACABADO

JRJ.2.3.2.4. NESTOR JALIMAO ACABADO, JR.

JRJ.2.3.3. FERNANDO JAMITO JALIMAO + WIFE SAN JUAN, W1 +
KENNY OJAS, W2 (Common Law)
JRJ.2.3.3.1. DAN MICHAEL SAN JUAN JALIMAO + WIFE SURNAME
JRJ.2.3.3.1.1. KIAN RAIN SAN JUAN JALIMAO + WIFE SURNAME
JRJ.2.3.3.2. FERNIE OJAS JALIMAO

JRJ.2.3.4. EFREN JAMITO JALIMAO + MARJORIE TAYABAS SABEROLA
JRJ.2.3.4.1. JEFREN SABEROLA JALIMAO
JRJ.2.3.4.2. JONATHAN SABEROLA JALIMAO
JRJ.2.3.4.3. MARY DEI SABEROLA JALIMAO
JRJ.2.3.4.4 . DONI DEUS SABEROLA JALIMAO
JRJ.2.3.4.5. MYCO AUROS SABEROLA JALIMAO, rip
JRJ.2.3.4.6. JOHN MERLIN SABEROLA JALIMAO
JRJ.2.3.5. FE JAMITO JALIMAO + JAIME SURETA GOYALA
JRJ.2.3.5.1 . RAYMOND JALIMAO GOYALA + WENILYN DELOS SANTOS
LEAÑO
JRJ.2.3.5.1.1. RAYCHELLE LEAÑO GOYALA
JRJ.2.3.5.1.2. WENCY REY LEAÑO GOYALA

JRJ.2.3.5.1.3. WILRENCE LEAÑO GOYALA

JRJ.2.3.5.2. JAIME JALIMAO GOYALA + MARIA RIZZA BARNEDO
JRJ.2.3.5.2.1 JAIRUZ BARNEDO GOYALA

JRJ.2.3.5.3. JESSIE JALIMAO GOYALA + RUTH DEREZ OGAD
JRJ.2.3.5.3.1 to follow

JRJ.2.3.5 4 . FEMY JALIMAO GOYALA

JRJ.2.3.5.5. JIMSON JALIMAO GOYALA

JRJ.2.3.5.6. JANE JALIMAO GOYALA

JRJ.2.3.5.7. MARIVIC JALIMAO GOYALA

JRJ.2.3.6. RAMON JAMITO JALIMAO + MYRNA RAVIZ VILLANUEVA
JRJ.2.3.6.1. MONALYN VILLANUEVA JALIMAO + LINO A. GOYALA
JRJ.2.3.6.1.1. RAYCHELLE LEAÑO GOYALA
JRJ.2.3.6.1.2. WENCY RAY LEAÑO GOYALA

JRJ.2.3.6.2 MARY ANN VILLANUEVA JALIMAO + HUSBAND SURNAME

JRJ.2.3.6.3. MICHELLE VILLANUEVA JALIMAO

JRJ.2.3.6.4. RAMON VILLANUEVA JALIMAO, JR.

JRJ.2.3.6.5 NIÑA VILLANUEVA JALIMAO

JRJ.2.3.7. EDWIN JAMITO JALIMAO, rip

JRJ.2.3.8. EVELYN JAMITO JALIMAO + ROLANDO ODEZA NAVA
JRJ.2.3.8.1 . CHARMAINE JALIMAO NAVA
JRJ.2.3.8.2 . KENNETH JALIMAO NAVA

JRJ.2.3.9. AMELIA JAMITO JALIMAO + JOSEPH BENAMIRA, SR.
JRJ.2.3.9.1. JOMELYN JALIMAO BENAMIRA
JRJ.2.3.9.2 . JOSEPH JALIMAO BENAMIRA, JR.

JRJ.2.3.9.3 . JAY JALIMAO BENAMIRA
JRJ.2.3.9.4.JOY JALIMAO BENAMIRA

JRJ.2.3.10. SIXTO JAMITO JALIMAO, JR. + MAY ANN GACHE IBIS
JRJ.2.3.10.1. KEISHA IBIS JALIMAO

JRJ.2.4. PLACIDO MATOLA JAMITO, rip + HELLEN, W1 + NORA, W2

JRJ 2.4.1. Enrique Jamito

JRJ.2.4.2. Sinnon Jamito

JRJ.2.4.3. Alexander Jamito

JRJ.2.4.4. No name

JRJ.2.4.5. Ismeraldo W2 Jamito

JRJ.2.5. PETRA MATOLA JAMITO + MARCIANO ADONES

JRJ 2.5.1. Bebot Jamito Adones, rip
JRJ.2.5.2. Ariel Jamito Adones
JRJ.2.5.3. Venus Jamito Adones
JRJ.2.5.4. Boy Jamito Adones
JRJ.2.5.5. Marife Jamito Adones

JRJ.2.6.JOSEFINA MATOLA JAMITO + LORETO LUSTRE

JRJ.2.6.1. Juanito Jamito Lustre + Maria Ginga
JRJ.2.6.1.1. Jonathan Ginga Lustre +Lyn Malingat
JRJ.2.6.1.1.1. Gabrielle Malingat Lustre

JRJ.2.6.1.2. Juanito Ginga Lustre Jr. + Me-Ann
JRJ.2.6.1.2.1. Ciara Mae Lustre
JRJ.2.6.1.2.2. Elizabeth Lustre
JRJ.2.6.1.2.3. Juana Lustre

JRJ.2.6.2. Renato Jamito Lustre + Rosemarie Montes
JRJ.2.6.2.1. Sherly Montes Lustre + Roden Fausto
JRJ.2.6.2.1.1. Sheryl Ann Grace Lustre Fausto
JRJ.2.6.2.1.2. Althea Sheryn Lustre Fausto
JRJ.2.6.2.2. Renan Jamito Lustre + Andrea
JRJ.2.6.2.2.1. Jan Karlo
JRJ.2.6.2.3. Joana Marie Jamito Lustre
JRJ.2.6.2.4. Raffy Jamito Lustre + Rachel Idea
JRJ.2.6.2.4.1. Sheryl Ann Grace Idea Lustre
JRJ.2.6.2.4.2.Althea Sheryn Idea Lustre

JRJ.2.6.2.5. Ronald Jamito Lustre +
JRJ.2.6.2.6. Rommel Jamito Lustre

JRJ.2.6.3. Erlinda Jamito Lustre + Edesser Malijan
JRJ.2.6.3.1. Lea Ann Lustre Malijan
JRJ.2.6.3.2.Rose Ann Lustre Malijan
JRJ.2.6.3.3.Bryan Anthony Lustre Malijan
JRJ.2.6.4. Arnolfo Jamito Lustre + Alicia Cabatsa
JRJ.2.6.4.1. Arjhay Cabatsa Lustre
JRJ.2.6.4.2.Arnold Cabatsa Lustre
JRJ.2.6.4.3.Karen Cabatsa Lustre

JRJ.2.7. DOLORES CASTILLO JAMITO + JOSE DAMIAN TAN

JRJ.2.7.1. JOEL JAMITO TAN + ROSALYN CASTANEDA ABAD
JRJ.2.7.1.1. NATHALIE GRACE ABAD TAN
JRJ.2.7.1.2. JOEL ABAD TAN
JRJ.2.7.1.3. STEPHANIE FAITH ABAD TAN and
JRJ.2.7.1.4. TIFFANY JOY ABAD TAN

JRJ.2.7.2. JENNIFER JAMITO TAN + HUSBAND SURNAME
JRJ.2.7.2.1. LOIS JOYCE TAN SURNAME

JRJ.2.7.3. JURIS JAMITO TAN + NOEL RAMIN ANDRES SANCHEZ
JRJ.2.7.3.1. NICOLE KELSEY TAN SANCHEZ
JRJ.2.7.3.2. ELIJAH JAMES TAN SANCHEZ

JRJ.2.7.3.3. JOHN NATHAN TAN SANCHEZ

JRJ.2.7.4. JANICE JAMITO TAN

JRJ.2.8. JULITA CASTILLO JAMITO + JOSE BASTO ESPANOL

JRJ.2.8.1. ESTRELLA JAMITO ESPANOL + PEDER ERIZXON
JRJ.2.8.1.1. SAMANTHA ESPANOL ERIXON

JRJ.2.8.2. DOMINADOR JAMITO ESPANOL + LEZYL
JRJ.2.8.2.1. LIZTER ESPANOL
JRJ.2.8.2.2. DOMINADOR ESPANOL JR

JRJ.2.8.3. EDUARDO JAMITO ESPANOL + BOTCH SEGUNDO
JRJ.2.8.3.1. ALEXANDER SEGUNDO ESPANOL
JRJ.2.8.3.2. ELENA SEGUNDO ESPANOL
JRJ.2.8.3.3. FATIMA SEGUNDO ESPANOL
JRJ.2.8.3.4. JEPOY SEGUNDO ESPANOL
JRJ.2.8.3.5. EDUARDO SEGUNDO ESPANOL JR.

JRJ.2.8.4. EMELITA JAMITO ESPANOL + JON DERRY, H2 + LING, H1
JRJ.2.8.4.1. CHRIS CHI CHUENG ESPANOL LING
JRJ.2.8.4.2. CLEVIN KIN CHUENG ESPANOL LING
JRJ.2.8.4.3. DANIEL CHUN CHUENG ESPANOL LING
JRJ.2.8.4.4. THOMAS PETER ESPANOL DERRY

JRJ.2.9. PACITA CASTILLO JAMITO + ERNESTO VELA MAGO

JRJ.2.9.1. EDUARDO JAMITO MAGO + FLOR MUNOZ MUIT
JRJ.2.9.1.1. CHRISTY MUIT MAGO
JRJ.2.9.1.2. CYRIL MUIT MAGO
JRJ.2.9.1.3. CINDY MUIT MAGO
JRJ.2.9.1.4. CHRISTIAN PAUL MUIT MAGO

JRJ.2.9.2. EDWIN JAMITO MAGO

Publisher - Tatay Jobo Elizes

JRJ.2.9.3. ELMER JAMITO MAGO
JRJ.2.9.4. EVELYN JAMITO MAGO
JRJ.2.9.5. JOJO JAMITO MAGO
JRJ.2.9.6. EFREN JAMITO MAGO
JRJ.2.9.7. ERIC JAMITO MAGO

JRJ.2.10. CRISTINA CASTILLO JAMITO + PEPITO E. MAGO, H1, rip + ALFREDO PANSACOLA, H2

JRJ.2.10.1. RONALDO J. MAGO+ ANALYN
JRJ.2.10.2. CYNTHIA J. MAGO
JRJ.2.10.3. FERDINAND J. MGO + MARIETTA
JRJ.2.10.4. MARYJANE J. MAGO + NILO MAGO
JRJ.2.10.5. FREDERICK J. MAGO + JENNIFER VELARDE
JRJ.2.10.6. MARICEL J. MAGO + CESAR TAMAYO
JRJ.2.10.7. MARICRIS J. MAGO + RONALDO
JRJ.2.10.8. MARITES J. MAGO
JRJ.2.10.9. ALCHRIS JAMITO PANSACOLA

JRJ.2.11. EUFRESINA CASTILLO JAMITO + GUILLERMO VERGARA

JRJ.2.11.1. ROWENA JAMITO VERGARA
JRJ.2.11.2. GEOFFREY JAMITO VERGARA
JRJ.2.11.3. RACHELLE JAMITO VERGARA
JRJ.2.11.4. EUGENE JAMITO VERGARA
JRJ.2.11.5. REGINE DANICA JAMITO VERGARA
JRJ.2.11.6. ROSE DIANE JAMITO VERGARA

JRJ.2.12. CRESENCIA CASTILLO JAMITO + FRANCISCO PASCUA,H1+ DIETER RUDOLPH, H2

JRJ.2.12.1. FLORENCE JAMITO PASCUA + JULIUS BUCALBOS
JRJ.2.12.1.1. JAN CHRISTIAN PASCUA BUCALBOS
JRJ.2.12.1.2. FRANCE DIETER PASCUA BUCLABOS

JRJ.3. EUGENIA RAGILES JAMITO + HUSBAND SURNAME

JRJ.3.1. ELYN JAMITO SURNAME + JOSE MUJAL *(former Daet Mayor candidate)*

JRJ.3.1.1. Children (List Not Available)

JRJ.4. PABLO RAGILES JAMITO - SINGLE *("KID JAMITO" as DAET BOXER CHAMPION)*

---oOo---

Note:

The above family tree listing is subject to correction by any member of this family. Please email the author and publisher for any corrections to incorporate in the revised edition of this book in the future. Thank you.

---oOo---

Publisher - Tatay Jobo Elizes

Publisher's List - <u>job_elizes@yahoo.com</u> or <u>tatay@usa.com</u>

#Writings 1 Book, 2009
I. **Catch That Story** - *Tatay Jobo Elizes, publisher*
II. **Obit** - *Bambi Harper, Famous columnist*
III. **Speech, UP, 2003** - *Butch Jimenez, PLDT Executive*
IV. **Speech, Silliman U, 2006** - *Butch Jimenez, PLDT Executive*
V. **The Mission Moment** - *Dr. Phil Stack, Psyhologist*
VI. **Writing Underground** - *Mila D. Aguilar, Poet & Writer*
VII. **Academic Freedom** - *Mila Aguilar, Poet & Writer*
VIII. **Subanon Spirits of Rice & Land** - *Noel Cornel Alegre, Acad.*
IX. **I Look Out The Window** - *Atty. Toto Causing, Lawyer, Journalist*
X. **Ride On A Bus, Poem** - *Anonymous via Melanie Ferrer, New Poet*
XI. **Why Am I Doing This** - *Susie Barbieri, Social Activist*
XII. **How To Court A Philipine Lady** - *Rodel Ramos & Jose Torres,*
XIII. **Inspiring Young Filipino Entrepreneur**-*Lloyd Luna, Motivator*
XIV. **The Success Story of Ian Del Carmen** - *Lloyd Luna, Motivator*
XV. **Story of Bacna Surgical Mission** - *Sylvia Salvador, Civics*
XVI. **1987 Philippine Constitution** - *Full Text (Special Feature)*
XVII. **Why Publish Writings** - *Tatay Jobo Elizes, Publisher*

Writings 2 Book, 2009
I. **Why Can't We Act Up Together** - *Susie Barbieri, Social Activist*
II. **I Know Where They Are All Going** - *Cesar Lumba, Writer & Poet*
III. **There Is Hope For The Philippines** - *Grace Padaca, Isabela Gov.*
IV. **Pointers On Employment Abroad** - *Melanie Aquino, Dentist*
V. **Without KNCHS: (Love story)** - *Atty. Toto Causing, Jury Proponent*
VI. **422 Years Ago** - *Rodel Rodis, Writer & Political activist*
VII. **Filipino American History Month** - *Rodel Rodis, Writer*
VIII. **Love is the Next Truth, poem** - *Daniel Rodis, son of Rodel*
IX. **A Need For Reflection - Gloom** - *Cesar Torres, Pol/academics*
X. **Our Purpose Driven Life** - *Joey Concepcion, RFM Pres. & GoNego*

XI. **Did Ninoy Die For Nothing** - *Joey Concepcion, RFM & GoNego*
XII. **Why The Filipino Voted** - *Pablito Lim, Zambales Businessman*
XIII. **Life And Love, Poem** - *Nannette Yatco, Dentist, Fine Artist, Poet*
XIV. **Criteria - American Institute of Philanthropy** - *Guidelines*
XV. **Strangers In Our Own Country** - *Casiano Mayor Jr., Author*
XVI. **Coming Revolution In The Ballot** - *Cesar Lumba, Author*
XVII. **2009 - A Retrospective** - *Cesar Lumba, Author & Writer*
XVIII. **All Over The World** - *Vicente Rivera Jr., Short Story Writer*
XIX. **Harvest** - *Loreto Paras Sulit, Short Story Writer*
XX. **Things Your Burglar Won't Tell** - *Jude Tagaciudad, Writer*
XXI. **The Gypsy Soul** - *Casiano Mayor Jr., Author & Writer*
XXII. **An End To Cheating** - *Sonny Coloma, Academician & Writer*
XXIII. **Toward Culture of Giving** - *Sonny Coloma, Academician*

Writings 3 Book, 2010

I. **EPIC25- Emerging Phil Investors Coalition**- *Norman Madrid, Eco.*
II. **Management Ability As An Issue** - *Dr. Rene B. Azurin, Academics*
III. **Do We Really Our Politicos More Power** - *Dr. Rene B. Azurin*
IV. **Will 2010 Fulfill High Hopes For Better Life** - *Ernie D. Delfin,*
V. **Comelec Is The Root Of All Evils** - *Toto Causing, Journalist*
VI. **Advantages of Fed/Parlia.** - *Dr. Jose Abueva, Ex-UP President*
VII. **Sometimes A Great Nation** - *Mar-Vic Cagurangan, Journalist*
VIII. **Great Conspiracy** - *Mar-Vic Cagurangan, Journalist*
IX. **Of Speech & Life's Riddles** - *Casiano Mayor, Author, journalist*
X. **Bad Start To The Year** - *Rod Garcia, Lawyer, composer, guitarist,*
XI. **A Dinner Out** - *Rod Garcia, Lawyer, composr, guitarist, poet*
XII. **One More Time** - *Roy Gaane, Writer*
XIII. **Musings** - *Ceres Busa, Writer*
XIV. **Value Formation For Good Citizenship** - *Roger Reyes, etc*
Ramon Gonzales + CDVictory + Mila Marzon, writers
XV. **On Being Filipino American** - *John Reyes, Writer*
XVI. **The Monterey Peninsula** - *John Reyes, Writer*
XVII. **The Salaza Fiesta** - *John Reyes, Writer*
XVIII. **Salawikain: Filipino Proverbs** - *John Reyes, Writer*
XIX. **Musikero (The Musician)** - *John Reyes, writer*
XX. **Strange Noises** - *Tatay Jobo Elizes, Publisher*

Writings 4 Book, 2010

I. **The State of Our Nation: Building 'The Good Society" We Want** *Dr. Jose V. Abueva, University President*
II. **Assessing Expanded Role of AFP** - *Col. Dennis Acop, Ret.*
III. **Assessing RP's Security Strategies** - *Col. Dennis Acop, Ret.*
IV. **The Way We Were** - *Fred Natividad, Accountant & Writer*
V. **Veterans of Ipo Dam, A Fiction** - *Fred Natividad, Accountant*
VI. **A Plea** - *Miguel Reyes Reynaldo, Historian*
VII. **Int'l Youth Bowling Impressions** – *Marjor Elizes Reyes, Teen*

Publisher - Tatay Jobo Elizes

VIII. **Mi Ultimo Adios (My Last Farewell)** - *Dr. Jose P. Rizal*
IX. **Aling Pagibig Sa Tinubuang Bayan** - *Gat. Andres Boniface*
X. **Rekonsilasyun Dula (Reunion in Heaven)** - *A Play By Irineo P. Goce (Kapule2 or Leonidas P. Agbayani), Writer and Playwright*
XI. **Forgery of Rizal Retraction** - *Irineo P. Goce (Kapule2)*
XII. **Maikling Kasaysayan Ng Malas Na Bayan** - *Ireneo P. Goce*

Writings 5 Book - "Best Hopes" 2010 (About PNoy)
I. **The Challenge of 100 Days: Believing that** - *Tony Meloto*
II. **The 2006 R. Magsaysay Award for Com. Serv.** - *for Tony Meloto*
III. **Open Letter to Noynoy** - *F. Sionil Jose, famous writer/author*
IV. **A History of Pain** - *Juan L. Mercado, Journalist*
V. **An Open Letter to Noynoy** - *From OFW'S*
VI. **Pursuit of Good Governance Advocacies** - *Marcelo Tecson, Fin.*
VII. **A Fervent Prayer for Peace** - *Cesar Torres, Academics*
VIII. **A History of Betrayal** - *Perry Diaz, Columnist*
IX. **Corona's Thorny Crown** - *Perry Diaz. Columnist*
X. **Dawn of a New Era** - *Perry Diaz, Columnist*
XI. **Of Mice, Boys and Men** - *Philip S. Chua, MD*
XII. **A Hopeful Tomorrow - A Balikbayan Insight** - *Philip S. Chua,*
XIII. **Global Filipinos: A Sleeping Giant** - *Philip S. Chua, MD*
XIV. **Heart to Heart - Winds of Change** - *Philip S. Chua, MD*
XV. **Growing Old is a Privilege** - *Philip S. Chua, MD*
XVI. **Our Cruelty to Mother Earth** - *Philip S. Chua, MD*
XVII. **Advice/Grads: "Never Choose Heroes Lightly"** - *Ernie Delfin*
XVIII. **Gawad Kalinga, A Progressive Movement** - *Ernie Delfin,*
XIX. **Why a Man Must Save and Invest** - *Ernie Delfin, writer*
XX. **Beautiful San Francisco, Pinoy Heaven** - *Ted Laguatan, lawyer*
XXI. **The President and PAMUSA** - *Frank Wenceslao, Pamusa Pres.*
XXII. **Philippne Budget Deficit** - *Frank Weneslao, Pamusa President*
XXIII. **Money Laundering: US Tools vs. Corrupt.** - *Frank Wenceslao*
XXIV. **Amid Fighting, Clan Rules Maguindanao** - *Jaileen F. Jimeno*
XXV. **Why I Publish Writings** - *Tatay Jobo Elizes, POD Publisher*

Writings 6 Book, 2010
I. **SONA - State Of Nation Address - English** - *Pres. B. Aquino III*
II. **SONA - State of Nation Address - Pilipino** - *Pres. B. Aquino III*
III. **First 100 Days Speech - Pilipino** - *Pres. Benigno Aquino III*
IV. **Finally, Another R. M. In The Making** - *Bert Guiang, USN, Ret.*
V. **A Covenant With Our President** - *Tony Meloto, GK Founder*
VI. **From A Grateful Heart - A Thank You Letter** - *Tony Meloto, GK*
VII. **The Scent of Hope For The Global Filipino** - *Tony Meloto, GK*
VIII. **Fleshing Out The Broad Strokes** - *Felicito (Tong) C. Payumo,*
IX. **In Search Of Leaders (Part1)** - *Felicito (Tong) C. Payumo, Ex-Cong*
X. **In Search of Leaders (Part 2)** - *Felicito (Tong) C. Payumo*
XI. **A Conspiracy of Dunces** - *Cesar Lumba, Writer, Blogger*

Writings 8 Book, 2010

Publisher - Tatay Jobo Elizes

XXVIII. **Sa Alaala ni Maria Lorena Barros** - *Percival Campoamor Cruz*
XXIX. **Text Game or Text Gambling?** - *Juan dela Cruz*
XXX. **Of Husbands and Wives** - *Juan dela Cruz*
XXXI. **It Must Be Love** - *Juan dela Cruz*
XXXII. **Elite Triad Blocking Reform** - *Demosthenes B. Donato*

Writings 9 Book, April 2011
I. **Solidarity in Literature Without Borders** - *Simeon Dumdum Jr*
II. **Macario Sakay Vindicated and Others** - *Gemma Cruz Araneta*
III. **The Dilemma of the Last Filipino** - *Larry Henares*
IV. **Ping Joaquin, Fil. Jazz Pianist, Loving Father** - *Tony Joaquin*
V. **Bert Del Rosario - Inventor of the Sing-Along** - *Tony Joaquin*
VI. **Xmas Article 2009** - *Allen Gaborro*
VII. **Beaches (short story)** - *Allen Gaborro*
VIII. **Democracy Versus Discipline** - *Allen Gaborro*
IX. **Amend the Const. Make Jury Trial** - *Toto C. Causing*
X. **Dakdak Beach Resort in Dapitan City** - *Toto C. Causing*
XI. **So I'm Dark-skinned, Leave Me Alone** - *Mar-Vic Cagurangan*
XII. **Dig My Sexy Flip Accent, Arizona** - *Mar-Vic Cagurangan*
XIII. **A Fan Mail From Prison** - *Mar-Vic Cagurangan*
XIV. **Three Poems: a. Please Don't Let Her Know, b. I Have Memories of My own c. God Has Made Someone Only For me** - *Emily Espanol Derry*
XV. **Three Love Poem: a. Some Good Things Never Last b. The Dance c. As I Trod Upon Your Ground** - *Elyn Jean Felarca*
XVI. **My Advocacy** - *by Naysan A. Albaytar*
XVII. **Feminism: The Great Paradox** - *Laura Wade*
XVIII. **A Blast From the Past** - *Peter Allan Mariano*
XIX. **Bus. Perspective: Building Your Future** - *Peter Allan Mariano*
XX. **An Overview of Health Connections** - *Peter Allan Mariano*
XXI. **My Workspace At Home** - *Marge Trajeco-Aberásturi*
XXII. **Investing on a Home Business** - *Marge Trajeco-Aberásturi*
XXIII. **A Brighter Day for Little Jane** - *Julia Carreon-Lagoc*
XXIV. **A Consummation Devoutly to Be Wished** - *Julia C. Lagoc*
XXV. **No Birds and Beetles and Trees** - *by Julia Carreon-Lagoc*
XXVI. **Ang Wika - Ang Tore Ni Babel Sa Pilipinas** - *Irineo Goce*
XXVII. **Scattered Thoughts** - *Anonymous*

Solo Authored Books:
Book A - **Turning Points - Empty Dreams** - *Job Elizes Sr,1968*
Book B - **Be Considerate - Behaviour Issues** - *Tatay Jobo Elizes (Jr)*
Book C - **Piglets Unlimited - Wealth Untapped** - *Tatay Jobo Elizes,*

Publisher - Tatay Jobo Elizes

Book D - **Out of the Misty Sea We Must** - *Cesar Lumba. 2010*
Book E - **Success Is A Journey** - *Cesar D. Candari, MD, 2010*
Book F - **Fulfilled** - *Gonzales Reynaldo, Editor, 2010*
Book G - **Reflections** - *Bert Guiang, 2010*
Book H - **Writings 7 - My Vintage Pics** - *Tatay Jobo Elizes, 2010*
Book I - **May Bagwis Ang Pag-ibig** - *Percival C. Cruz, 2010*
Book J - **Letters To Matrimony** - *Irineo Perez Coce, Ka Pule2, 2011*
Book K - **Songs I Wish You Knew** - *Poems of Soledad R. Juan, 2011*
Book L - **Make My Day** - *Hilarion (Larry) Henares Jr., 2011 re-issue*
Book M - **Our Guerrero Family** - *Tatay Jobo Guerrero Elizes, 2010*

Publisher - Tatay Jobo Elizes